Architect's Job Book
Fifth edition 1988

Volume 1: Job Administration
Volume 2: Contract Administration
Job Record

Compiled by
Leonard Beaven
Stanley Cox
David Dry
Roderick Males

Fifth edition 1988
Reprinted 1989, 1991, 1993

©RIBA Publications Ltd

Published by
RIBA Publications Ltd
Finsbury Mission, 39 Moreland Street, London EC1V 8BB

ISBN 0 947877 32 0 (soft covers)
ISBN 0 947877 29 0 (loose-leaf)

Printed by
Jolly & Barber Ltd, Rugby, Warwickshire

Architect's Job Book: Volume 2
Fifth edition 1988

CONTRACT ADMINISTRATION

RIBA Publications

Contents

The Fifth Edition
How to Use Volume 2: Contract Administration

Contents

Contents

Architect's Job Book:
Fifth edition 1988

The new edition consists of:

Volume 1: Job Administration
Volume 2: Contract Administration
Job Record

These three items may be bought as a package, or separately. All may be bought 'off the shelf' at the RIBA Bookshops at 66 Portland Place, and in Bristol and Manchester, or by mail order from:

RIBA Publications Ltd, Finsbury Mission,
39 Moreland Street, London EC1V 8BB.

Volume 1   Job Administration

Job Administration is essentially a reference book, arranged under the RIBA *Plan of Work* stages. It contains guidance, checklists and specimen letters and forms. Each stage begins with *Action checklists* followed by *'Watchpoints'* – commonsense reminders and caveats in a less formal style.

The headings used for the *Action checklists* are maintained throughout the work stages and are also used to structure design team and other meetings so as to maintain administrative coherence and continuity whilst the job is in progress.

Typical letters and forms are included under each work stage together with practical advice, reminders and caveats.

Job Administration is cross-referenced throughout with its sister shelf book, **Contract Administration**. Used together, the two books present a comprehensive understanding of effective project management.

Volume 2   Contract Administration

Volume 2 gives advice on selecting the most suitable procurement path and form of contract and offers comprehensive guidance on administering contracts. It includes related specimen letters, instructions and forms, together with practical advice and useful references. It will be recognised as a successor to the popular 'White Book' *(A Guide to Contract Administration for Architects)*, which was published in 1971 to complement the *Handbook of Architectural Practice and Management.*

The format differs from **Job Administration**. In each chapter there is general comment on the matters listed under headings, followed by detailed comment specifically relating to the three principal forms of contract published by the Joint Contracts Tribunal:

· the Standard Form of Building Contract 1980 Edition
  (JCT 80)

· the Intermediate Form of Building Contract for Works of Simple Content 1984 Edition
  (IFC 84)

· the Agreement for Minor Building Works 1980 Edition
  (MW 80)

The text includes reference to JCT amendments published up to the date of going to press.

Numerous cross-references are made into **Volume 1, Job Administration**, which is similarly cross-referenced back into **Volume 2**.

Scots Law
There is no express reference to Scottish law or to the forms produced by the Scottish Building Contract Committee. Although much of the contents of this book is readily applicable, readers should always check the position for themselves if they are in any doubt.

Job Record

The **Job Record**, as its name implies, is essentially a vehicle for recording information, as distinct from **Volumes 1** and **2** which are related reference books. It is a 'skeleton' pad of blank forms, registers, charts etc where all the basic information and events relating to a project from start to finish may be noted.

If the relevant **Job Record** forms are selected and properly completed for each project, architects will have an invaluable set of condensed project histories for future reference.

How to use Volume 2: Contract Administration

The book is divided into seven chapters which correspond broadly with the section headings now used by the Joint Contracts Tribunal for its recent main forms of contract. (Section headings were first introduced in MW 80 and were adopted for the later Intermediate Form, IFC 84, and the Management Contract 1987.) This format is intended for future editions of other existing forms.

Integration

Contract administration is not a matter of separate and self-contained procedures, and architects will need to refer frequently to Volume 1, **Job Administration**. Decisions on many things which contribute significantly to the smooth running of a contract have to be taken early in the pre-contract stage.

In this book, matters which concern specialist sub-contractors, named or nominated, are included in Section 3. This section deals generally with sub-contracting (or 'sub-letting', the traditional term used in the Standard Form, JCT 80).

It was decided not to include any detailed reference to arbitration, although many architects are likely to be asked by employers to advise on or explain the arbitration clauses, since this is not directly a matter of contract administration. Specialist guidance on the subject should be sought elsewhere. The Bibliography may help.

Comments

Each chapter begins with a section of general comment. This is not to be taken as a legal commentary; architects who wish to be reminded about contract principles should read an appropriate text. Again, refer to the Bibliography.

Detailed comments follow which specifically relate to the three most widely used forms of contract published by the Joint Contracts Tribunal:

·   the Standard Form of Building Contract 1980 Edition
    (JCT SF80, commonly referred to as 'JCT 80'*)

·   the Intermediate Form of Building Contract for Works of Simple Content 1984 Edition **(IFC 84)***

·   the Agreement for Minor Building Works 1980 Edition
    (MW 80)*

These comments are not intended to provide a full commentary on the forms; they highlight matters which are of direct concern to the person actually running the job.

*   The abbreviations used throughout this book.

Abstracts from the clauses

Where appropriate, abstracts follow which give the actual words or phrases used in the clauses, so that architects can check which actions are required and which are empowered. For points of detail the full version of the clause or clauses in question should be studied.

'Watchpoints'

These offer commonsense advice and observations and are informal in style.

The 'specimen' forms and letters

These are models to be adapted to suit particular circumstances. Never use any of them without properly assessing the particular situation you are dealing with. The *context* is all-important. However busy you are, *never* photocopy a specimen letter, fill in the project details and send it out. Examples are there to help you to see how facts should be marshalled and presented and what style, approach and attention to detail is needed. They can be a useful part of the process of solving a problem; they are not solutions in themselves. Refer also to the Introduction (*0.6 Contractual correspondence*).

References

Each chapter ends with a list of references to Practice or Procedure Notes, and other notes or material published by three bodies:

·   the Joint Contracts Tribunal (JCT)

·   the National Joint Consultative Committee (NJCC)

·   the Royal Institute of British Architects (RIBA)

These items are easily obtained, but architects should check whether any revisions or amendments to them have been published recently.

Appendices

The appendices contain supplementary information about preparing the contract documents.

Bibliography

A short bibliography is included of standard texts and titles for general reading and information.

Introduction

0

The term 'contract' signifies the binding together of two or more persons over a common intention. A contract is an agreement which is intended by the parties to give rise to obligations which are enforceable at law. Where one party is in breach of his obligations, the other may seek to enforce performance of them or claim compensation in the courts.

Volume 1
A2.1 Action checklists
A2.2 'Watchpoints'
A3 Negotiating
Appointment

Under a building contract, the contractor undertakes to carry out work in return for a sum of money paid by the employer.* These are the two parties to the contract. Parties may be individuals or legal entities which may be incorporated as a company, unincorporated as a partnership, club or society, or joined as trustees. It is important that the identity and nature of the parties to a contract are clearly established at the outset.

The terms of building contracts should be set out clearly in writing, although this is not a legal requirement. At its simplest, this is effected by an exchange of letters, which may incorporate conditions by reference. However, the terms of building contracts tend to be complex, and it makes sense to use standard forms which have been drafted by experts. These are available for most types of building contracts.

0.1.1 JCT Forms of Contract

Forms of contract published by the Joint Contracts Tribunal are unique in that they are documents agreed with the bodies representing general contractors, specialist contractors and sub-contractors, employers and the professions. JCT forms are more widely used than other forms, and are generally accepted and understood by tenderers. They are accepted by the Courts as fair and balanced between the parties, provided they are current editions which have not been subject to unauthorised amendments. Amendments are issued by the JCT from time to time, and these should be incorporated.

0.1.2 The Contract Documents

Make sure that the information on which the accepted tender is based is the same information as that carried in the contract documents. This is sometimes overlooked when last minute changes are made. Inevitably a subsequent corrective instruction is needed, or there may be a claim or, worse still, a dispute.

Volume 1
B2 Developing the Brief
F5 Tendering Procedures –
Documentation

Consider carefully which descriptive documents are to become contract documents. There will usually be drawings, but the appropriate manner in which other essential information is carried in bills of quantities, specifications or schedules will depend on the particular job and the terms of the contract. All the documents should

---

*   By a metamorphosis of terminology, long accepted in the building industry and by the legal profession, the architect's 'client' is called the 'employer' in the building contract.

be free from error, ambiguity or conflict. This compatibility is of course also needed between contract documents and documents issued later to amplify or explain the work.

Take care when making the necessary entries to the form of contract, in the Articles of Agreement, Recitals, Articles and Appendix. Be clear whether or not option clauses are to apply. Vague or conflicting entries or spaces left blank do not help to establish the agreed intentions of the parties.

0.1.3 Sub-contracts

The terms of a main contract are not automatically imported into any sub-contract. There is often an express requirement in main contracts for the use of specific forms for some sub-contracts to ensure a close correlation with the main contract conditions. The main contract may also require the contractor to ensure that certain conditions appear in his domestic sub-contract forms.

Volume 1
A2.1 Action checklists
A2.2 'Watchpoints'

As a rule, only the parties to a contract (or their lawful assignees) have rights and duties arising from that contract. (In contract law this is known as 'privity of contract'.) Collateral agreements are necessary to bring others into a contractual relationship, to enable rights and duties outside of the main contract to be enforced. This is particularly valuable where specialist sub-contractors or suppliers have design or performance responsibilities which are outside the main contract obligations.

0.2   The Architect as Contract Administrator

Architects who are RIBA members, or in partnership with RIBA members, and who act as contract administrators have general duties and obligations under the following:

Volume 1
Checklist Figs A3.1.3,
A3.1.4, A3.1.5

RIBA Code of Professional Conduct

Rule 1.4

'A member shall act impartially in all cases in which he is acting between parties. Where he has responsibilities as architect under a building contract, or is acting for the supervising officer, he shall interpret the conditions of such contract with fairness.'

Rule 2.3

'A member shall not and shall not purport to carry out the independent functions of an architect or of a supervisory officer in relation to a contract in which he or his employer is the contractor.'

RIBA Guidelines for Sound Practice

Guideline 2.5

Building contract
'Considering appropriate forms – A recommendation should be based on the client's requirements. The consequences of choice should be understood by all parties.'

Guideline 2.6

Construction documentation
'Administering the contract – Standard aids should be used to develop sound policies for tendering and contract administration purposes.'

RIBA Architect's Appointment

Description of Basic Services, in particular agreement to:

Para 1.21

Administer the terms of the building contract during operations on site.

Para 1.22

Visit the site as appropriate to inspect generally the progress and quality of the work.

Para 1.24

Administer the terms of the building contract relating to the completion of the works.

Description of other services which might be undertaken in addition to the Basic Services and of which the following might be particularly relevant:
Project management (2.38)
Design and build contracts (2.39)
Separate trades contracts (2.40)
Direct labour (2.41).

'Watchpoints'

The precise role of the architect as contract administrator will depend on the terms of the appointment and upon the authority stated in the conditions of the particular building contract. However, there are some practical watchpoints to bear in mind:

✻ Investigate and advise on the appropriate procurement path and contract type at an early stage, preferably feasibility.

Volume 1
Action checklist
B2.1 (70)
B2.2 'Watchpoints'

✻ Make sure that the type of contract recommended and the form of contract selected are compatible. Make an early decision about the information on which the contract is to be based and by what means it will be conveyed. Check clarity and consistency in and between the various documents.

✻ Read the form of contract and make sure you understand what it requires of you. Check that it is the intended edition, that it includes the latest improvements or amendments and that selected supplements have been properly incorporated. Check what relevant ancillary documents, if any, are to be used.

Volume 1
Action checklist
B2.1 (70)
B2.2 'Watchpoints'

✻ Make sure that the contract form is completed properly, with option clauses clearly marked and appendix entries completed in full. Check that the contract is correctly executed and try to have all documents signed, sealed or initialled as appropriate before work starts on site.

✻ Establish clear responsibilities with the contractor at the outset for such matters as site supervision, site management and programming. Agree a policy for issuing Architect's Instructions, site visits, progress meetings and communication generally. Agree with consultants clear procedures and lines of communication always through the architect.

Volume 1
J4 Briefing Site
Supervisory Staff
J6 Initial Project Meeting

✻ Remember that implied terms may also exist in addition to the express terms in the contract.

✻ Follow the rules and procedures laid down in the building contract meticulously. They have been designed to assist contract administration and are contractual obligations.

✻ Be fair, decisive and timely wherever the contract requires action or where the contractor might otherwise be unable to fulfill his obligations. Avoid the risk of claims and of allegations that the employer is in breach of contract through you.

✻ Do not exceed the authority stated in the contract conditions. Where the contract refers to agreement by the employer it means precisely that. If the employer wishes you to act for him, get this confirmed in writing.

Volume 1
K2.1 Action Checklists
K2.2 'Watchpoints'
K3 Keeping the Client Informed
K4 Meetings on Site
K6 Running the Contract

✻ Keep accurate records of all important discussions, visits, decisions and instructions. You might need to refer to them not only during the life of the contract, but also throughout the defects liability period.

Choosing the appropriate form of building contract should not and often cannot be tackled until the procurement path and the type of contract have been established.

Volume 1
Action checklists
B2.1 (70), F2.1 (70)

The following factors will be influential:

1 **The type of work**
(whether new building and extensions, refurbishment and major alterations, maintenance and minor repair work).

2 **The type of operation**
(whether mainly building work, largely civil engineering work, landscaping, interior design, etc).

3 **The time factor**
Is there enough time to prepare full documentation before tenders are invited? Is time for construction limited and/or subject to key dates?

4 **Design team**
The extent to which consultants are to be involved, and their anticipated roles and responsibilities.

5 **The nature of the work**
The likely cost, complexity, extent to which specialist skills will be needed.

6 **The scope of the work**
Can this be accurately determined at pre-contract stage? Are there likely to be significant changes required as the work progresses?

7 **The design factor**
Is the design down to fine detail a crucial aspect of the work? Can it be developed as the work proceeds?

8 **The cost**
Must the contract figure be accurate? Does the employer have to keep to a strict budget? Is he subject to stringent accountability?

9 **Early appointment of contractor**
Would the involvement of a contractor at pre-contract stage be beneficial? Can the work be undertaken on a negotiated basis, or must it be competitive?

10 **The risk factor**
How are the risks to be apportioned? Is the employer willing to accept some increased costs arising from damage, unexpected hazards, shortages, adverse weather, etc? Is the contractor expected to bear the risks and price accordingly?

0.3.1 The Procurement Path

The procurement path will influence the appointment of consultants and their responsibilities. It will also influence the method and timing of the contractor's appointment and the extent of his responsibilities. The procurement paths usually adopted are:

1 Traditional
Consultants are appointed for design and cost control. The contractor is appointed by competitive tender on complete information, or earlier by negotiation on partial or notional information, for example by using separate contracts either preliminary or in parallel.

2 Design and build
Consultants are appointed to advise the employer on his requirements. The contractor is appointed either by competitive tender or by negotiation. Responsibility may be for total design and construction, preferably on the basis of a fully worked out set of requirements from the employer, or it may be for design development and production information on the basis of a scheme design supplied by the employer.

Fig 0.3.1   **New building (including extensions)**

Item	Documents	Forms available
1 Traditional		
(a) Lump sum	Drawings + firm quantities	JCT 80 (With Q), IFC 84
	Drawings + specification	JCT 80 (Without Q), IFC 84, MW 80
	Drawings + schedules of work	JCT 80 (Without Q), IFC 84
(b) Measurement	Drawings + approximate quantities	JCT 80 (Approx Q)
2 Design		
Design and build	Employer's requirements (written)	JCT CD 81
Develop and construct	Scheme design + employer's requirements	JCT CD 81
Contractor's designed portion	Drawings + quantities	JCT 80 + CDPS 81
3 Management		
Management contracting	Project drawings, project specification, contract cost plan	JCT Standard Form of Management Contract 1987
	Drawings, specifications, bills of quantities	JCT Standard Form of Works Contract 1987

3 Management

Consultants are appointed for design and cost control. The management contractor is appointed on a fee basis to manage construction and to place all work through separate trades contracts (ie management contracting). Alternatively, the management contractor may be appointed on a fee basis to manage the construction, but all separate trades are placed directly by the employer (ie construction management). The management contractor may also be responsible for the management of design and cost control.

0.3.2 Types of Contract

1 Traditional Procurement

Traditional procurement path contracts are for work and materials only. Under these contracts responsibility for design is limited to what is implied by the obligation to conform with the contractual requirements for standards and quality of workmanship and materials and to comply with Building Regulations and other statutory requirements in order to realise the design given to the contractor under the contract. The contractor undertakes to carry out and complete the work as shown or described on the documents supplied by the employer. As a rule, the contractor is responsible for workmanship and materials, and this extends to the workmanship and materials of all sub-contractors, regardless of status. The contractor will be responsible for all defects which arise, except those which can be directly attributed to faulty design of the work which the contractor was required to execute.

(a) Lump sum contracts
The contractor undertakes to carry out a defined amount of work in return for an agreed sum. Lump sum contracts 'with quantities' are based on drawings and priced bills of quantities. Lump sum contracts 'without quantities' are based on drawings and either a specification or schedules of work. (A schedule of rates or a contract sum analysis is usually needed as a priced document if the contract document is not sufficiently detailed to enable the contractor to price it.)

Contracts can be based on bills of *notional* quantities where parallel working for large projects of long duration is necessary. However a lump sum contract will not be possible until the notional bills are replaced by bills of firm quantities later. Otherwise the use of approximate quantities will result in a measurement contract.

Lump sum contracts can be used with serial tendering for a series of broadly similar jobs. The successful tenderer's rates form a standing offer for the whole series. A separate lump sum contract is necessary for each job in the series.

Lump sum contracts can be used for two stage tendering where urgency requires the early selection of a contractor on an agreed basis, followed later by a negotiated lump sum.

Lump sum contracts can be used for 'continuation' or 'run-on' contracts after a negotiated tender is accepted from a contractor already carrying out similar work for the employer on the same site. A separate lump sum contract is usual.

Lump sum contracts on a 'joint venture' or 'consortium' basis are often let on standard conditions. The only difference lies in the specially created legal identity of the contractor.

(b) Measurement contracts

Sometimes referred to as 're-measurement' contracts.

The contractor undertakes to carry out an amount of work which cannot for good reasons be accurately measured pre-contract. The cost is ascertained by measurement and valuation related to a schedule which is included in the contract.

Measurement contracts can be based on drawings and bills of approximate quantities. This is appropriate where the type of work is known, but the quantity cannot be measured accurately. The work is measured as the contractor proceeds and is valued at the rates in the contract bills.

Fig 0.3.2   Refurbishment (including major alterations)

Item	Documents	Forms available
1 Traditional (a) Lump sum	Drawings + firm quantities	JCT 80 (With Q), IFC 84
	Drawings + specification	JCT 80 (Without Q), IFC 84, MW 80
	Drawings + schedules of work	JCT 80 (Without Q), IFC 84
(b) Measurement	Drawings + approximate quantities	JCT 80 (Approx Q)
	Drawings + specification + schedules	JCT Fixed Fee Prime Cost 1976
	Drawings + schedule of rates	Adapt MW 80
2 Design Develop and construct	Scheme design + employer's requirements	JCT CD 81
3 Management Management contracting	Project drawings, project specification, contract cost plan	JCT Standard Form of Management Contract 1987
	Drawings, specifications, bills of quantities	JCT Standard Form of Works Contract 1987

Measurement contracts can be based on drawings and a schedule of rates. This is appropriate where the quantity is so uncertain that not even approximate quantities can be prepared, or where there is no time to prepare them.

Measurement contracts for maintenance work are often term contracts. The contractor undertakes to do work of a particular kind in a particular area or over a particular period of time. The precise requirements are often not known until the work needs to be done. The contractor is usually appointed after competitive tendering on the basis of a schedule of rates with percentage adjustments for each job, according to its value category.

Cost reimbursement contracts, sometimes referred to as *cost plus* contracts, are measurement contracts. The contractor undertakes to carry out an indeterminate amount of work for a sum of money to be ascertained on the basis of the actual costs incurred. To these recorded costs is added a fee which is to cover overheads, including management, and profit. The prime cost elements are not too difficult to establish and include costs directly related to the works (eg labour, plant, materials). The fee to cover head office costs, overheads and profit, etc is the variable and can be agreed before the contract is let on several different bases.

In a *cost plus fixed fee* contract, the fee is fixed by the contractor at tender stage. This is appropriate where the amount of work can be estimated reasonably well. The contractor has an incentive to work efficiently in order to remain within his fee.

In a *cost plus percentage fee* contract, the fee is related to the total prime cost. It is sometimes on a sliding scale, in proportion to the total cost rather than a flat rate percentage. Thus the contractor has no real incentive to work efficiently. This type of contract will only be appropriate where requirements are difficult to ascertain pre-contract, as with some maintenance work.

In a *cost plus fluctuating fee* contract, the fee fluctuates inversely according to the actual prime cost compared with the estimated cost. As the prime cost increases, the amount of the fee decreases. The contractor has an incentive to work efficiently.

In a *target cost* contract, the contractor is paid the prime cost plus a fixed fee which is based on an agreed target cost. Any difference between the actual prime cost and the target cost, whether it is extra or a saving, is shared between the employer and the contractor on a pre-arranged basis. This is often difficult to operate.

In a *value cost* contract, the contractor is paid only an agreed fee. The cost of operations (eg labour, materials, plant charges, etc) is paid direct by the employer. This is a type of contract used mainly by large organisations with a continuous work programme.

2 Design and Build Procurement

Under a traditional building contract, a contractor has an implied duty to warn the employer where he has real doubts concerning the design and matters of buildability. The contractor is responsible for his working methods and for the design of temporary formwork and falsework. He might have some responsibility for the fitness of materials, components and construction where there has clearly been reliance upon his specialist knowledge and skill. However, under a work and materials contract he is not liable for matters of general design.

The design and build procurement path requires the use of a contract where the design responsibility is expressly included. Unless a Clause which reduces the design liability has been included, this responsibility will be absolute – the contractor undertakes to produce a building fit for the purpose intended. This is usually the situation in package deals or turnkey contracts, where no independent consultant has been directly involved in the design.

However, many design and build contracts do expressly limit the contractor's design liability to that of exercising reasonable skill and care. This matches the normal professional liability of professionals engaged by contractors to prepare their designs.

It is possible for the contractor to accept design liability for some part of the work otherwise carried out under a traditional work and materials contract, for example, piling, suspended flooring, roof trusses. This can be done by incorporating a supplement in the main contract. It is wise to establish the extent of the design liability beforehand, particularly if some decisions have already been made by consultants.

Fig 0.3.3   **Maintenance (and minor repair work)**

Item	Documents	Forms available
1 Traditional		
(a) Lump sum	Drawings/specifications/schedules (one-off minor contract of repair and maintenance)	Adapted MW 80
(b) Measurement	Drawings + specification/schedules	JCT Fixed Fee Prime Cost 1976
	Drawings/schedules	Term Maintenance Contract✷
	Drawings/specification/schedule of rates	Measured Term Contract✷
		✷No standard forms are yet available from JCT
2 Design	Not applicable	
3 Management	Not applicable	

Similarly, the design liability of the contractor in a *develop and construct* contract, where key design decisions have already been taken by consultants, needs to be clearly established beforehand. The respective liabilities of contractor and consultants are often difficult to define precisely but nevertheless should be attempted.

3 Management Procurement

The contractor joins the professional team at an early stage in order to contribute his unique knowledge of the industry's methods and his expertise in labour management, programming and site operations. He is paid a consultant's fee and has a direct contractual relationship with the employer.

The management contractor does not carry out the building work in 'management contracting'. This is done by contractors directly responsible to him under a series of separate trades or works contracts. (In 'construction management' the works contracts are directly between the works contractors and the employer.)

Where (very unusually) the management contractor is permitted to carry out certain building work himself, the arrangement is sometimes referred to as a 'managing contract'.

The following are the most common forms of contract for use by architects listed under the contract types previously described.

1 Lump sum

JCT 80

Published by the Joint Contracts Tribunal
Standard Form of Building Contract (JCT 80)
Local Authorities With Quantities (with Amendments)
Private With Quantities (with Amendments)
Local Authorities Without Quantities (with Amendments)
Private Without Quantities (with Amendments)

Supplements available to cover:
Sectional Completion
Fluctuations
Formula Rules
Contractor's Designed Portion

Ancillary documents for nominated sub-contractors and suppliers:
NSC/1 to NSC/4
NSC/1a to NSC/4a
TNS/1 and TNS/2

IFC 84

Intermediate Form of Building Contract (with Amendments)

Supplements available to cover:
Sectional Completion
Fluctuations and Formula Rules

Ancillary documents for named sub-contractors:
NAM/T and NAM/SC
ESA/1

MW 80

Agreement for Minor Building Works (with Amendments)
Agreement for Renovation Grant Works
(where architect is employed)
Agreement for Renovation Grant Works
(where architect is not employed)

ACA

Published by the Association of Consultant Architects
Form of Building Agreement (ACA/2)
Form of Building Agreement (ACA/BPF)

FAS

Published by the Faculty of Architects & Surveyors
Building Contract (1986 Edition)
Small Works Contract (1981 Edition)
Minor Works Contract (1980 Edition)

GC/Works

Published by HMSO for Central Government Contracts
Form GC/Works/1 (General Conditions only)
Form GC/Works/2 (General Conditions only)

2   Measurement

JCT 80

Published by the Joint Contracts Tribunal
Local Authorities with Approximate Quantities
(with Amendments)
Private with Approximate Quantities (with Amendments)

ICE

Published by the Institution of Civil Engineers
The ICE Conditions of Contract (5th Edition)

3   Cost reimbursement

Fixed Fee

Published by the Joint Contracts Tribunal
Fixed Fee Form of Prime Cost Contract (1976 revision)

4   Design and build

CD 81

Published by the Joint Contracts Tribunal
Standard Form With Contractor's Design (with Amendments)

5   Management

SFMC

Published by the Joint Contracts Tribunal
Standard Form of Management Contract 1987
Works Contract/1 (section 1: invitation to tender,
                              section 2: tender, section 3: Articles)
Works Contract/2 (Conditions)
Works Contract/3 (Employer/Works Contractor Agreement)

Supplements available to cover:
Phased completion – Management Contract
Phased completion – Works Contract

Building contracts refer to the issue of instructions, valuations, certificates etc, but do not usually stipulate what form these must take. Under certain circumstances letters can be construed as instructions or even certificates. It is therefore wise to agree at the outset what form these important communications should take.

Volume 1
Action checklists
J2.1(70), K2.1(70),
L2.1(70)

Architects are recommended to use the range of contract administration forms produced especially for use with JCT contracts (published by RIBA Publications Ltd). They are convenient and, used properly, can help to reduce the risk of error and ambiguity.

Letters will still be needed where for example the architect is simply consenting to a proposal by the contractor, or where a warning is being sounded. But whenever the architect is communicating a decision which requires action in compliance, it is wise to issue an Architect's Instruction. This will preferably indicate the cost implications, if any, or state that the instruction is at no extra cost to the employer. The consistent use of Architect's Instructions in all appropriate circumstances rather than letters also has the practical advantage that the records of such matters of decision are all filed in one place.

It is important that the appropriate administration forms are used for a particular contract, and that they are of recent date to be consistent with Clause references etc. Pads of forms can have far too long a shelf life, and should be regularly checked to make sure that they are current.

Care should be taken over distribution. Whether or not the particular administration form has a printed box indicating that copies should be sent to various parties, it is essential to keep the employer, quantity surveyor, appropriate consultants and, where necessary, nominated specialist firms informed. It is equally important that a clerk of works also receives copies.

Where the form is to be sent to the contractor, it is wise to agree at the outset the most efficient lines of communication. It is often necessary to send simultaneously to the contractor's office, and to the contractor's organisation on site to avoid unnecessary delay.

Architect's Instruction

For use with JCT 80,
IFC 84, MW 80

Only the architect is empowered to issue instructions under the contract and this should be made clear to the contractor, especially where other consultants are retained or a clerk of works is employed. Instructions must be in writing. A contractor acting on unconfirmed oral instructions or directions from the clerk of works does so at risk. Such directions have no effect until confirmed in writing by the architect, and this must be within two working days (Clause 12).

The Architect's Instruction form should be used for matters which involve adjustments to the contract sum and for those which do not.

The Architect's Instruction form includes provision for the approximate valuation of the work and for a running estimate of the adjusted contract sum. This cost information is for the benefit of the employer and, depending on the administrative policy adopted for the project in the interests of the employer, the architect may decide to include it in the employer's copy of the instruction only.

Architect's Instructions are issued to the contractor, with copies to the employer, quantity surveyor, other consultants, nominated sub-contractors and clerk of works as appropriate. Each Instruction should be dated, numbered in sequence and referenced.

Issued by:
address:

Architect's instruction

Employer:
address:

Serial no:

Job reference:

Contractor:
address:

Issue date:

Contract dated:

Works:
Situated at:

Under the terms of the above Contract, I/We issue the following instructions:

SPECIMEN

	Office use: Approx costs
	£ omit	£ add

To be signed by or for
the issuer named
above.

Signed _____

Amount of Contract Sum	£	
± Approximate value of previous instructions	£	
	£	
± Approximate value of this instruction	£	
Approximate adjusted total	£	

Distribution ☐ Employer   ☐ Contractor   ☐ Quantity Surveyor   ☐ Services Engineer

☐   ☐ Nominated
Sub-Contractors   ☐ Structural Engineer   ☐ File

Clerk of Works Direction

For use with JCT 80

The powers of the clerk of works are limited. The clerk of works is employed solely as an inspector on behalf of the employer, under the direction of the architect. The clerk of works may only give directions in relation to matters over which the architect may issue instructions. Even so, these directions have no authority unless confirmed in writing by the architect within two working days (Clause 12).

To maintain a proper record, the Clerk of Works Direction form should be used for all directions issued. Directions should be dated and numbered in sequence. The original (ie the signed top copy) should be handed to the contractor's site representative, a copy should be sent immediately to the architect, and a copy should be retained on site. An Architect's Instruction confirming a Clerk of Works Direction should refer to the date, reference and serial number of the Direction.

Architect/CA:
address:

Clerk of works direction

Employer:
address:

Serial no:

Job reference:

Contractor:
address:

Issue date:

Contract dated:

Works:
Situated at:

Original to Contractor

Under the terms of the above Contract, I issue the following direction.

This direction shall be of no effect unless confirmed in writing by the Architect/the Contract Administrator within 2 working days and does not authorize any extra payment.

Direction	Architect/CA use

Covered by
Instruction No:

Signed _____ Clerk of works

Notification of an Extension of Time

For use with IFC 84,
MW 80

Under IFC 84 the contractor is required to give written notice to the architect forthwith if it becomes 'reasonably apparent' that the progress of the works is or is likely to be delayed. He is required to give notice of the cause of delay and provide whatever information may be reasonably necessary for the architect to consider the application (Clause 2·3).

If the architect considers that completion of the works has been delayed or is likely to be delayed he must, as soon as he is able to estimate the length of delay, make a fair and reasonable extension of time in writing (Clause 2·3), stating the event under which the extension is being made.

Under MW 80 the architect is required to make a reasonable extension of time in writing if it becomes apparent that the works will not be completed by the completion date for reasons beyond the control of the contractor (Clause 2·2).

Although not a requirement of the contracts, the architect would be wise to state the grounds upon which the extension of time is being granted on the Notification of an Extension of Time form. It should be issued to the employer dated, referenced and numbered. Copies should be sent to the contractor, clerk of works, quantity surveyor and other consultants as appropriate.

Notification of an

Extension of time

Issued by:
address:

Employer:
address:

Serial no:

Contractor:
address:

Job reference:

Issue date:

Works:
Situated at:

Contract dated:

Under the terms of the above mentioned Contract,

I/We give notice that the time for completion is extended beyond the Date for Completion stated in the Contract so as to expire on:

_____ 19_____

To be signed by or for the issuer named above.

Signed _____

Distribution

Original to:	Duplicate to:	Copies to:	
☐ Employer	☐ Contractor	☐ Quantity Surveyor	☐ Services Engineer
		☐ Structural Engineer	☐ File

Notification of Revision to Completion Date

For use with JCT 80

The contract provides for the architect to revise the contract completion date before practical completion in response to an application by the contractor (Clause 25·3·1), and also within the 12 weeks following the issue of the Certificate of Practical Completion as the result of the architect's review of any 'relevant events', whether or not the matter has been raised previously (Clause 25·3·3)). Under alternative (a), the architect may wish to carry out this review after the completion date and before practical completion (Clause 25·3·3).

The form may be used for revisions made prior to practical completion (alternative a) and for revisions made after it (alternative b). Revisions made before practical completion can only result from formal applications by the contractor (Clause 25·2). Where the architect considers that a revision is not fair and reasonable, the contractor must be notified to that effect (Clause 25·3·1). Revisions made after practical completion may result from the architect's review of the circumstances relating to any relevant event, whether formally notified by the contractor or not (Clause 25·3·3·1).

The contractor is required to notify any nominated sub-contractor referred to in an application (Clause 25·2·1 and 25·2·3), and the architect is required to notify all nominated sub-contractors of any revision to the completion date (Clause 25·3·5).

The Notification, dated, referenced and numbered, is issued to the contractor, and copies sent sent to the employer, clerk of works, all nominated sub-contractors, quantity surveyor and other consultants as required.

Notification of
revision to
Completion date

Issued by:
address:

Employer:
address:

Contractor:
address:

Works:
Situated at:

Contract dated:

Serial no:

Job reference:

Issue date:

Under the terms of the above mentioned Contract,

I/We give notice that the Completion Date previously fixed as

_____ 19_____

*Delete as appropriate

*is hereby fixed later than that previously fixed;

*is hereby fixed earlier than that previously fixed;

*is hereby confirmed;

and is now

_____ 19_____

†Statement (a) is for revisions made **prior** to Practical Completion and (b) for revisions **after** Practical Completion. Delete as appropriate.

(a) †by reason of the relevant events identified in the Contractor's notices, particulars and estimates, and/or instructions requiring as a variation omission of work, which are set out below/overleaf;

(b) †by reason of our review pursuant to clause 25·3·3.

To be signed by or for the issuer named above.

Signed _____

Distribution	Original to:	Duplicate to:	Copies to:	
	☐ Contractor	☐ Employer	☐ Quantity Surveyor	☐ Services Engineer
		☐ Nominated Sub-Contractors	☐ Structural Engineer	☐ File

© 1985 RIBA Publications Ltd

Certificate of Partial Possession by the Employer

For use with JCT 80,
IFC 84

Although JCT 80 includes provisions for the employer to take possession of part of the work before practical completion of the whole of the works, these should be used with caution. In effect, the issue of the certificate marks the practical completion of the part concerned, which the employer then becomes responsible for and may occupy. The part taken over is known as the 'relevant part', and the date of issue of the certificate is known as the 'relevant date'.

The employer may only take possession of part of the works with the agreement of the contractor, but the contractor's agreement may not be unreasonably withheld.

Practical completion of the relevant part is deemed to have taken place on the relevant date and the customary procedures of practical completion apply to the relevant part. The defects liability period on the relevant part runs from the relevant date (Clause 18·1·1). Only half of the retention percentage applies to the relevant part and this is released on the issue of the Certificate of Completion of Making Good Defects (Clause 30·4·1·3).

IFC 84 provides an optional partial possession Clause, as described in Practice Note IN/1. The intention to include partial possession should be stated at the time of tendering, although if phased completion appears to be the goal, then the Sectional Completion Supplement should be used.

The Certificate, dated, numbered and referenced, is issued to the employer, with copies to the contractor, nominated sub-contractors, clerk of works, quantity surveyor and other consultants as required.

Certificate of

**Partial
possession**

by the Employer

Issued by:
address:

Employer:
address:

Serial no:

Contractor:
address:

Job reference:

Issue date:

Works:
Situated at:

Contract dated:

Under the terms of the above mentioned Contract,

I/We certify that a part of the Works, referred to as the relevant part, namely:

_____

_____

the approximate value of which I/we estimate for the purposes of this

Certificate, but for no other purpose, to be . . . . £ _____

was taken into possession by the Employer on:

_____ 19_____

and that for this relevant part of the Works only the Defects Liability

Period will end on:

_____ 19_____

To be signed by or for
the issuer named
above.

Signed _____

Distribution	Original to:	Duplicate to:	Copies to:	
	☐ Employer	☐ Contractor	☐ Quantity Surveyor	☐ Services Engineer
		☐ Nominated Sub-Contractors	☐ Structural Engineer	☐ File

Certificate of Non-completion

For use with JCT 80,
IFC 84, MW 80

Under JCT 80 (Clause 24·1) and IFC 84 (Clause 2·6) the architect is required to issue a certificate if the contractor fails to complete the works on the date for completion stated in the contract, or the revised or extended date for completion.

MW 80 does not include provision for the issue of such a certificate, but it is good practice for the form to be used so that the parties are aware of their rights and obligations.

Certificate of

Non-completion

Issued by:
address:

Employer:
address:

Contractor:
address:

Works:
Situated at:

Contract dated:

Serial no:

Job reference:

Issue date:

Under the terms of the above mentioned Contract,

I/We certify that the Contractor has failed to complete the Works by the Date for Completion or within any extended time fixed under the contract provisions.

To be signed by or for the issuer named above.

Signed_____

Distribution

Original to:	Duplicate to:	Copies to:	
☐ Employer	☐ Contractor	☐ Quantity Surveyor	☐ Services Engineer
		☐ Structural Engineer	☐ File

© 1985 RIBA Publications Ltd

Certificate of Practical Completion of the Works

For use with JCT 80,
IFC 84, MW 80

The architect is required to certify practical completion of the works
when he considers that this has been achieved. The issue of the
Certificate of Practical Completion marks a significant stage in the
contract and is important that the parties understand its
implications.

The Certificate fixes the date of the beginning of the defects liability
period, and the contractor becomes responsible for making good
defects, shrinkages or other faults which appear during the defects
liability period and which are due to materials or workmanship not in
accordance with the contract. Although the defects liability period is
normally six months in the case of JCT 80 and IFC 84 and three
months in the case of MW 80, other periods may apply. The architect
should check the period stated in the Appendix before completing
the form.

It is important to note that the contracts make no provision for
issuing a qualified Certificate of Practical Completion. The whole of
the works must have achieved practical completion before the
Certificate can be issued. Difficulties are likely to arise from ad hoc
modifications to the certificate, and the rights of the parties may be
infringed. Where only minor items are still outstanding, procedures
for partial possession could be considered.

The certificate may be used in connection with work to which the
Sectional Completion Supplement applies.

The Certificate, dated, referenced and numbered, is issued to the
employer with copies to the contractor and nominated
sub-contractors, clerk of works, quantity surveyor and other
consultants as required.

Certificate of

Practical Completion

of the Works

Issued by:
address:

Employer:
address:

Contractor:
address:

Works:
Situated at:

Contract dated:

Serial no:

Job reference:

Issue date:

Under the terms of the above mentioned Contract,

I/We certify that Practical Completion of the Works was achieved on:

_____ 19_____

To be signed by or for the issuer named above.

Signed_____

The Defects Liability Period will therefore end on:

_____ 19_____

Distribution

Original to:	Duplicate to:	Copies to:	
☐ Employer	☐ Contractor	☐ Quantity Surveyor	☐ Services Engineer
	☐ Nominated Sub-Contractors	☐ Structural Engineer	☐ File

**Certificate of Practical Completion of Nominated
Sub-contract Works**

For use with JCT 80   The architect is required to certify the practical completion of each of
the nominated sub-contract works (Clause 35·16). The nominated
sub-contractor notifies the contractor when he believes that practical
completion of the nominated sub-contract works has been achieved
and the contractor is required to forward this notification to the
architect, making whatever observations he wishes (NSC4, or
NSC4a, Clause 14·1). The architect is then required to consider the
notification and determine whether or not practical completion has
been achieved.

The Certificate is issued to the employer, with copies to the contractor
and nominated sub-contractor, clerk of works, quantity surveyor and
other consultants as required.

Practical
Completion of

Nominated
Sub-Contract
Works

Issued by:
address:

Employer:
address:

Contractor:
address:

Serial no:

Job reference:

Works:
Situated at:

Issue date:

Contract dated:

Nominated
Sub-Contract
Works:

Under the terms of the above mentioned Contract,

I/We certify that:

Practical Completion of the Nominated Sub-Contract Works referred to above, was achieved on:

_____ 19_____

To be signed by or for the issuer named above.

Signed_____

Distribution	Original to:	Duplicate to:	Copies to:	
	☐ Employer	☐ Contractor	☐ Quantity Surveyor	☐ Services Engineer
		☐ Nominated Sub-Contractors	☐ Structural Engineer	☐ File

Certificate of Completion of Making Good Defects

For use with JCT 80,
IFC 84, MW 80

The contractor may be required to make good defects, shrinkage or
other faults which appear during the defects liability period and arise
from materials or workmanship not in accordance with the contract
or from frost occurring before practical completion.

The architect is required to issue a schedule of these defects within
14 days of the end of the defects liability period and the contractor is
required to make good the defects within a reasonable period.

Where the architect considers it necessary, instructions may be
issued for defects to be made good during the defects liability period
under JCT 80. No such provision for emergency work appears in
IFC 84 or MW 80, but it would be reasonable for the work to be
done by agreement during the defects liability period. Instructions
for making good such defects may not be issued after the delivery of
the schedule of defects or after the 14 day period following the end
of the defects liability period.

The form includes an alternative (2) which applies to making good
defects on parts of the works which have been subject to partial
possession under JCT 80 (Clause 18) and under IFC 84 where the
optional Clause described in Practice Note IN/1 is in use. It is
important that the extent of work covered by the partial possession
certificate is properly defined in order that the matters referred to in
the schedule of defects may be clearly identified.

The dated, referenced and numbered Certificate is issued to the
employer, with copies to the contractor, clerk of works, quantity
surveyor and other consultants as required.

Certificate of
completion of

**Making good
defects**

Issued by:
address:

Employer:
address:

Serial no:

Contractor:
address:

Job reference:

Issue date:

Works:
Situated at:

Contract dated:

Under the terms of the above mentioned Contract,

I/We hereby certify that the defects, shrinkages and other faults specified
in the schedule of defects delivered to the Contractor as an instruction have
in my/our opinion been made good.

This Certificate refers to:

*1. The Works described in the Certificate of Practical Completion

Serial no._____dated_____

*2. The Works described in the Certificate of Partial Possession of a relevant

part of the Works

Serial no._____dated_____

*Delete as
appropriate

To be signed by or for
the issuer named
above.

Signed_____

Distribution

Original to:	Duplicate to:	Copies to:	
☐ Employer	☐ Contractor	☐ Quantity Surveyor	☐ Services Engineer
	☐ Nominated Sub-Contractors	☐ Structural Engineer	☐ File

© 1985 RIBA Publications Ltd

Certificate of Progress Payment

For use with MW 80

Certificates of Progress Payment have to be issued at intervals of not less than four weeks, if requested by the contractor (Clause 4·2).

The employer is required to pay the contractor within 14 days of the issue of the Certificate (Clause 4·2). The architect should advise the employer that its issue is imminent and that payment is required within 14 days.

The amount certified is for the value of the work properly carried out including any amounts arising from variations (Clause 3·6), the expenditure of provisional sums (Clause 3·7) and the value of goods and materials properly delivered to the site and properly protected (Clause 4·2).

The retention amount is 5% of the total value unless otherwise agreed. This reduces to 2.5% on the issue of the 'penultimate certificate', which should take place within 14 days of the issue of the Certificate of Practical Completion. Payment of the balance of the retention money is included in the Final Certificate.

The Minor Works form makes no reference to the distribution of copies of Progress Payment Certificates, but it is suggested that the original (ie the signed top copy) should be issued to the employer, and a signed duplicate sent to the contractor. A copy may be sent to the quantity surveyor, if any. The Certificates should be dated, numbered in sequence and referenced.

The Minor Works form has no provision for partial possession or for payments for off-site goods and materials.

Certificate of

**Interim/
Progress
payment**

Issued by:
address:

Employer:
address:

Serial no: **A**

Contractor:
address:

Certificate no:

Job reference:

Works:
Situated at:

Issue date:

Valuation date:

Contract dated:

Original to Employer

This certificate for interim/progress payment is issued under the terms

of the above mentioned Contract in the sum of £ _____

A: Value of work executed and of materials and goods on site

(excluding items included in B below) . . . . £ _____

[1] Percentage is normally 95% except where Practical Completion has been achieved (97½%) or where some other percentage has been agreed by the parties.

1   Amount payable at_____%   . . . . £ _____

[2] Space has been left for special payments such as at 'partial possession' and for goods and materials off site.

2   £ _____

[3] This item applies only to IFC 84 Conditions and should be deleted where the Contract is MW 80. See Notes on the use of this form.

3   B: Amounts payable (or deductible) in accordance with IFC 84

clause 4·2·2 at 100% . . . . £ _____

Sub-total   £ _____

Less amounts previously certified . . . . £ _____

Amount for payment on this Certificate . . . . £ _____

I/We certify that the amount for payment by the Employer to the

Contractor on this Certificate is (in words)

_____

_____

All amounts are exclusive of VAT

To be signed by or for the issuer named above.

Signed_____

Contractor's provisional assessment of total amounts included in above

certificate on which VAT will be chargeable £_____ @_____%

This is not a Tax Invoice

© 1986 RIBA Publications Ltd

Certificate of Interim Payment

For use with IFC 84

Interim valuations are made whenever the architect considers them necessary for the ascertainment of amounts due in interim payments. The valuation must take place not more than seven days before the date of issue of the Certificate of Interim Payment. Certificates have to be issued at intervals of one month calculated from the date of possession, unless otherwise agreed in the Appendix (Clause 4·2).

The employer is required to pay the contractor within 14 days of the issue of the Certificate (Clause 4·2). The architect should advise the employer that its issue is imminent and that payment is required within 14 days.

The amount certified is for the value of the work properly carried out including any amounts arising from variations (Clause 3·7); the expenditure of provisional sums (Clause 3·7); formula fluctuations (Clause 4·9); and the value of goods and materials properly delivered to the site and properly protected (Clause 4·2).

Apart from the matters referred to below which are not subject to retention, the retention amount is 5% of the total value unless otherwise agreed. This reduces to 2.5% on the issue of the Certificate of Interim Payment, which should take place within 14 days of the issue of the Certificate of Practical Completion. Payment of the balance of retention money is included in the Final Certificate.

Retention does not apply to costs arising from the inspection of work (Clause 3·12); fixed price fluctuations of tax etc (Clause 4·9); fluctuations on named persons' work (Clause 4·10); disturbance of progress (Clause 4·11); statutory obligations (Clause 5·1); and insurance premiums (Clauses 6·3B and 6·3C·1). These items must be listed and shown separately on an addendum to each certificate until the Final Certificate.

The Certificate for Interim Payment may also make deductions at 100% of costs in connection with reductions on fluctuations of tax etc (Clause 4·9); reductions of fluctuations on named persons' work (Clause 4·10); and deductions made in connection with errors in setting out (Clause 3·9).

The certificate form leaves space for special payments in connection with 'partial possession' and 'goods or materials off-site' at item 2. If these optional procedures, which require the agreement of the parties to the contract, are adopted, the details of the value inserted should be itemised on an addendum to the certificate.

Unless otherwise agreed, the Certificate for Interim Payment, dated, numbered and referenced, is signed and issued to the employer, and a signed copy is sent to the contractor. A copy may be sent to the quantity surveyor, if any.

Certificate of

Interim/
Progress
payment

Issued by:
address:

Employer:
address:

Serial no: **A**

Contractor:
address:

Certificate no:

Job reference:

Works:
Situated at:

Issue date:

Valuation date:

Contract dated:

Original to Employer

This certificate for interim/progress payment is issued under the terms

of the above mentioned Contract in the sum of £_____

A: Value of work executed and of materials and goods on site

(excluding items included in B below) . . . . £ _____

[1] Percentage is normally 95% except where Practical Completion has been achieved (97½%) or where some other percentage has been agreed by the parties.

1   Amount payable at_____% . . . . 1 £ _____

2   £ _____

[2] Space has been left for special payments such as at 'partial possession' and for goods and materials off site.

3   B: Amounts payable (or deductible) in accordance with IFC 84

[3] This item applies only to IFC 84 Conditions and should be deleted where the Contract is MW 80. See Notes on the use of this form.

clause 4·2·2 at 100% . . . . £ _____

Sub-total £ _____

Less amounts previously certified . . . . £ _____

Amount for payment on this Certificate . . . . £ _____

I/We certify that the amount for payment by the Employer to the

Contractor on this Certificate is (in words)

_____

_____

All amounts are exclusive of VAT

To be signed by or for the issuer named above.

Signed_____

Contractor's provisional assessment of total amounts included in above

certificate on which VAT will be chargeable £_____ @_____%

This is not a Tax Invoice

© 1986 RIBA Publications Ltd

Interim Certificate and Direction

For use with JCT 80

Interim valuations are made whenever the architect considers them necessary for the ascertainment of amounts due in interim payments. The valuation must take place not more than seven days before the date of issue of the Interim Certificate (Clause 30·2). Certificates have to be issued at the intervals stated in the Appendix or, if no interval is stated, every month up to and including the period during which the Certificate of Practical Completion is issued. Thereafter Interim Certificates are issued as necessary, but at not less than monthly intervals (Clause 30·1·3).

The gross amount certified is for the value of the work properly carried out to the relevant date including any amounts arising from work by nominated sub-contractors; variations; the expenditure of provisional sums; and the value of goods and materials properly delivered to the site and properly protected (Clause 30·2·1). In addition, goods and materials prepared for the works which are stored off-site may be included in the valuation at the discretion of the architect, on condition that they are complete, have been set apart, are clearly identified and marked, properly stored and protected, fully insured, and that the interests of the employer in the goods and materials are properly safeguarded (Clause 30·3).

Apart from the matters which are not subject to retention, the retention amount is 5% of the total value unless otherwise agreed. This reduces to 2.5% on the issue of the Certificate of Practical Completion. Payment of the balance of retention money is included in the Final Certificate.

Interim Certificates which include work by nominated sub-contractors must be accompanied by a Statement of Retention and of Nominated Sub-contractors' Values (Clause 35·13·1). The architect is required to notify nominated sub-contractors of sums due to them under Interim Certificates.

The amounts shown on Interim Certificates exclude VAT, but provision is made for the contractor's provisional estimate of the proportion of the amount certified on which VAT may be chargeable. The Interim Certificate is not acceptable as a tax invoice.

The Interim Certificate, dated, numbered and referenced, is signed and issued to the employer, and a signed duplicate is sent to the contractor. A copy may be sent to the quantity surveyor, if any. The contractor's copy is also marked as a Direction drawing attention to the Contractor's obligation to make payments to the nominated sub-contractors listed on the Statement of Retention and of Nominated Sub-contractors' Values.

The Interim Certificate is not appropriate for use as a Final Certificate.

Interim certificate

and Direction

Issued by:
address:

Employer:
address:

Contractor:
address:

Works:
Situated at:

Contract dated:

Serial no: **B**

Interim Certificate no:

Job reference:

Issue date:

Valuation date:

Original to Employer

Under the terms of the above mentioned Contract, in the sum of

£ _____

I/We certify that interim payment as shown is due from the Employer to
the Contractor, and

I/We direct the Contractor that the amounts of interim or final payments due
to Nominated Sub-Contractors included in this Certificate and listed on the
attached *Statement of Retention and of Nominated Sub-Contractors' Values*
are to be discharged to those named.

Gross valuation inclusive of the value of Works by Nominated
Sub-Contractors . . . . £

Less Retention which may be retained by the Employer as detailed on
the Statement of Retention . . . . £ _____

Sub-total £

Less total amount stated as due in Interim Certificates previously

issued up to and including Interim Certificate no: £ _____

Amount for payment on this Certificate . . . . £ _____

(in words)_____

_____

All amounts are exclusive of VAT

To be signed by or for
the issuer named
above.

Signed_____

Contractor's provisional assessment of total amounts included in above

certificate on which VAT will be chargeable £_____@_____%

This is not a Tax Invoice

**Statement of Retention and of Nominated Sub-contractors'
Values**

For use with JCT 80

Where Interim Certificates include payments due to nominated sub-
contractors, it is necessary for a detailed Statement of Retention and
of Sub-contractors' Values to accompany each certificate. Copies of
the Statement should also be issued, together with the form of
Notification, to each of the nominated sub-contractors concerned
(Clause 35·13·1).

The Statement makes provision for the gross valuation of work by
the contractor and also by each of the nominated sub-contractors;
the identification of amounts subject to full retention (in the case of
work for which the Certificate of Practical Completion has not been
issued), half retention (in the case where the Certificate of Practical
Completion has been issued) and nil retention (in the case where the
Certificate of Practical Completion has been issued and defects have
been made good); and the calculation of amounts of retention and
balances due.

All nominated sub-contractors have to be listed on the Statement,
but in order to maintain confidentiality only the relevant name should
be shown on the copy sent to each nominated sub-contractor.

Statements must be dated, referenced and related to the relevant
Interim Certificates. Where a quantity surveyor is engaged, it is usual
for his valuation to be accompanied by a completed statement which
may use the RIBA form or the similar form prepared by the RICS.

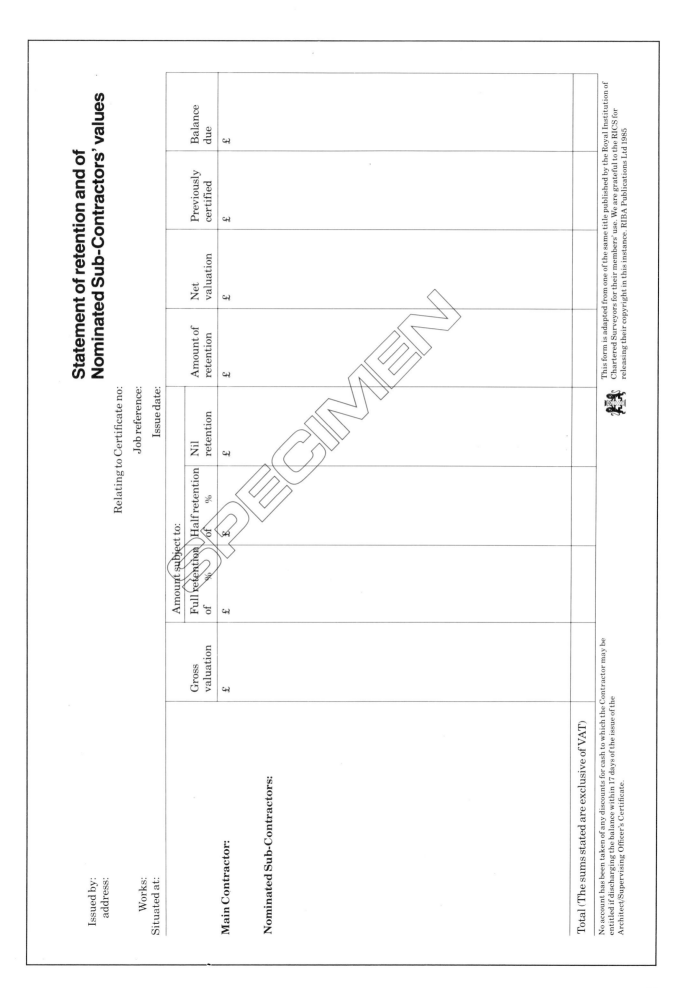

Statement of retention and of Nominated Sub-Contractors' values

Issued by:
address:

Works:
Situated at:

Relating to Certificate no:

Job reference:

Issue date:

	Gross valuation	Amount subject to:			Amount of retention	Net valuation	Previously certified	Balance due
		Full retention of %	Half retention of %	Nil retention				
	£	£	£	£	£	£	£	£
Main Contractor:								
Nominated Sub-Contractors:								
Total (The sums stated are exclusive of VAT)								

No account has been taken of any discounts for cash to which the Contractor may be entitled if discharging the balance within 17 days of the issue of the Architect/Supervising Officer's Certificate.

This form is adapted from one of the same title published by the Royal Institution of Chartered Surveyors for their members' use. We are grateful to the RICS for releasing their copyright in this instance. RIBA Publications Ltd 1985

51

**Notification to Nominated Sub-contractor concerning
Amount included in Certificates**

For use with JCT 80   Where Interim Certificates include payments due to nominated sub-
contractors, the architect is required to notify them of the amounts
due (Clause 35·13·1). Each nominated sub-contractor is notified in
the Notification form, together with the relevant Statement of
Retention and of Nominated Sub-contractors' Values. The form
should be issued at the same time as the Interim Certificate to which
it refers.

The Notification form includes an Acknowledgement of Discharge
proforma which the nominated sub-contractor is to complete and
return to the contractor when payment has been made. The
contractor may use this as evidence to the architect that payments
have been discharged as directed. The returned acknowledgements
should be carefully recorded and filed.

Issued by:
address:

Employer:
address:

Contractor:
address:

Works:
Situated at:

Contract dated:

Nominated
Sub-Contractor:
address:

Notification
to Nominated
Sub-Contractor
concerning amount
included in certificates

Serial no:

Job reference:

Issue date:

Valuation date:

Original to Nominated
Sub-Contractor

*Delete as
appropriate

Under the terms of the above mentioned Contract, I/we inform you that an interim/a final* payment due to you of £_____ has been included in Interim Certificate no._____ dated_____ issued to the Employer, and that the Contractor named above has been directed in the said Certificate to discharge his obligation to pay this amount in accordance with the terms of the Contract and the relevant Sub-Contract. Where applicable, retention has been deducted but no account has been taken of any discounts for cash to which the Contractor may be entitled.

To comply with your obligation to provide written proof of discharge of the certified amount, you should return the acknowledgement slip below to the Contractor immediately upon such discharge.

To be signed by or for
the issuer named
above.

Signed_____

Contractor:
address:

Works:
Situated at:

Nominated Sub-Contractor's
**Acknowledgement
of discharge**
of payment due

Job reference:

Notification date:

Interim Certificate Serial no:

We confirm that we have received from you discharge of the amount included in Interim Certificate Serial no:_____ dated_____ as stated in the Notification dated_____

in accordance with the terms of the relevant Sub-Contract.

Signed_____ Nominated Sub-Contractor

Date_____

Final Certificate

For use with JCT 80, IFC 84, MW 80

Although the same Final Certificate form may be used for all three JCT contracts, there are some differences in the procedures involved.

JCT 80

The architect is required to issue the Final Certificate within two months (unless otherwise agreed in the Appendix) of the latest date of the following events: the end of the defects liability period; the completion of making good defects; or the receipt by the architect of all the necessary documents from the contractor for the adjustment of the contract sum. The architect is required to notify each nominated sub-contractor of the date of the issue of the Final Certificate. Payment is due 28 days after the date of the Final Certificate (Clause 30·8).

IFC 84

The architect is required to issue the Final Certificate within 28 days of the contractor sending the computation of the adjusted contract sum to the architect (Clause 4·5), or 28 days of the architect's issue of the Certificate of Completion of Making Good Defects, whichever is the latest. Payment is due 21 days after the date of the Final Certificate (Clause 4·6).

MW 80

The architect is required to issue the Final Certificate within 28 days of the receipt of all the necessary documents from the contractor for the adjustment of the contract sum, provided that the Certificate of Completion of Making Good Defects has been issued. The contractor is required to provide the information within three months from the date of practical completion, unless otherwise agreed. Payment is due 14 days after the date of the Final Certificate (Clause 4·4).

The balance shown on the Final Certificate may be due to the contractor from the employer, or to the employer from the contractor, and it is important that this is clearly indicated and the appropriate phrase deleted.

Amounts shown on the Final Certificate exclude VAT. The Final Certificate is not acceptable as a VAT invoice.

The Final Certificate, signed and completed, is issued to the employer, with copies to the contractor and quantity surveyor.

Issued by:
address:

Employer:
address:

Contractor:
address:

Works:
Situated at:

Contract dated:

Final Certificate

Serial no:

Job reference:

Issue date:

Original to Employer

Under the terms of the above mentioned Contract,

the Contract Sum adjusted as necessary is . . . . £

The total amount previously certified for payment to the contractor is . . . £

The difference between the above stated amounts is . . . . £

(in words)_____

_____

_____

*Delete as appropriate

and is hereby certified as a balance due* to the Contractor from the

Employer/*to the Employer from the Contractor.

All amounts are exclusive of VAT

To be signed by or for the issuer named above.

Signed_____

*Delete as appropriate

1   The terms of the Contract provide that the amount shall as from the

*14th/21st day after the date of this Certificate be a debt payable from the

one to the other subject to any amounts properly deductible by the

Employer.

This is not a Tax Invoice

Note:

1 Payment becomes due 14 days after issue where the contract is JCT 80 or MW 80 and 21 days after issue for IFC 84.

© 1985 RIBA Publications Ltd

Reminders

Letters, AIs, site meeting minutes and notes of inspections etc associated with contract works are part of the story of that contract and, if there is any subsequent investigation connected with litigation, they will be part of the evidence. Therefore it is crucial that they are clearly expressed and unambiguous. Many disputes arise simply because letters and instructions are misunderstood. Here are some points to remember.

Use a formal style
· Letters connected with contractual matters are always formal. Start and end them 'Dear Sir – Yours faithfully'.
Be sure to refer to yourself as 'we', not 'I'.

Get the references right
· The main heading will be the name of the contract works and any project number. Always date the document as the date of issue, not the date it was drafted.

State the relevant Clause in the contract
· Quote the Clause number in the contract that relates to the subject of the letter or AI with the name of the form of contract or sub-contract under which the works are being carried out. ('This request is made in accordance with (relevant Clause) of IFC 84.')
Check that you have got it right.

Quote drawing numbers correctly
· It is equally important to quote drawing numbers and their titles exactly and fully.

Refer to events precisely
· State the relevant date and where necessary the location.

Keep sentences short and language simple
· Contract provisions are often expressed in a convoluted way and this tends to creep into the rest of the correspondence.

Remember to send copies to all the relevant parties
· Some architects believe in copying all job-related correspondence to the client as a matter of course. You *must* copy all contract-related correspondence to him or her.

Finally, three golden rules:

1 **Consult your solicitor**
Be sure to do this whenever a situation arises where there may be legal repercussions; he or she will advise you in the light of the particular circumstances.

2 **Advise your insurers**
Similarly, you must advise your insurers immediately of any circumstances likely to give rise to a claim. Failure to notify in good time can be a valid reason for their refusal to indemnify.

3 **Don't ignore claims**
Respond if claims or allegations are made, but always take legal advice about the form of your reply.

Intentions of the Parties

1

'Watchpoints'

References

JCT

Practice Notes
4: JCT 80 - Drawings - Additional Copies
7: SFBC for use with Approximate Quantities
20: Deciding on the appropriate form (revised July 84)
23: A Contract Sum Analysis
IN/1: The Contract Documents, p3

NJCC

Procedure Notes
2: Alterations to Standard Forms
3: Additional Information for Tenderers
13: Naming of Quantity Surveyor etc

Guidance Notes
1: Joint Venture Tendering 1985
2: Performance Bonds 1986

Codes of Procedure
for Single Stage Tendering
for Two Stage Tendering

RIBA

Practice Notes
JCT Standard Form: 1980 (RIBAJ February 1980 p13)
JCT Agreement for Minor Works: 1980 (RIBAJ March 1980 p11)
Naming the architect in articles of agreement
(RIBAJ June 1980 p56)
Use of Agreement for Minor Works
(RIBAJ August 1980 p91)
JCT Standard Form 'With Contractor's Design': 1981 edition
(RIBAJ November 1981 pp 67, 69)
Use of JCT 63 (RIBAJ February 1982 p53)

'Practice'
JCT 80 Amendments (April 1984 p8)
Introduction to JCT Intermediate Form (October 1984 p1)
IFC 84 Contract Documentation (December 1984 p1)
Preliminaries for IFC 84 (February 1985 p7)
Standard Forms of Building Contract: Current Issues
(June 1985 p3)
Coordinated project information (CPI) (June 1987 p5)
Keeping drawings and files (June 1987 p11)
Selecting the appropriate JCT Form of Contract (July 1987 p2)

The contractor is obliged to carry out and complete the works as shown and described in the contract documents. It is therefore essential to identify exactly what they constitute. The scope, quantity and quality of the works should be clearly described in them.

The contract documents are the core of the agreement between the parties and, in the event of a dispute, the first point of reference. Their preparation is not a mere formality. They should be consistent and should adequately describe the works and the standards required under the contract.

The physical boundaries of the site of the works should be clearly shown, and any restrictions to be imposed on the contractor should also be included.

Information issued subsequently is limited to amplifying or explaining the information the contract documents contain.

Unless otherwise agreed, the architect is responsible for issuing and circulating copies of contract documents and other supplementary information. The circulation list, procedures for distributing and recording information on site and in the office and any special requirements should be agreed at the initial project meeting and confirmed in writing. Unless otherwise determined, all information prepared by consultants and other specialists should be issued through the architect.

It is usual for copies of contract documents, other contract instructions and drawings to be issued to the clerk of works, the quantity surveyor and all other consultants. The employer may also require copies of all instructions and drawings issued, especially in the case of local authorities and other public clients.

Information issued under Architect's Instruction forms will constitute a clear, continuous and consistent record of information, and the use of AIs is strongly recommended. Letters may be suitable for works of very small scale, or in special circumstances (*see Introduction: Forms for contract administration*).

Contractors sometimes request additional copies of documents on large contracts, far beyond the numbers provided as free issue. In such circumstances the employer may agree to additional free issues. If not, the contractor should be charged and invoiced monthly by the architect or the consultant responsible for originating them. The contractor should of course also expect to pay for drawings needed for the purposes of sub-contract quotations and work.

Volume 1
J6 Initial Project Meeting
Specimen agenda Fig K4.1
Action checklist J2.1 (70)

This Volume
Intro 0.5

JCT 80

Clause 2·1

The contractor is required to carry out and complete the works in accordance with the contract documents, which will specify the materials, workmanship, quality and standards required. The architect may reserve the right to approve materials and workmanship; quality and standards must then meet with his reasonable satisfaction, and eventually the issue of the Final Certificate will be conclusive proof. When specifying, it is generally advisable to limit those parts of the works which are to be subject to the architect's approval to superficial matters where the possibility of latent defects does not arise.

Clause 5·2

Immediately after the contract has been signed, the architect must provide the contractor with a certified set of contract documents, two further sets of contract drawings, two copies of unpriced bills of quantities (or schedules or specification as appropriate). These may be issued under an Architect's Instruction or letter, or be handed over at the pre-site meeting, and this fact confirmed in the minutes.

Clause 5·5

The contractor is required to keep one set of documents and any further drawings or details on site for the architect to refer to.

> Immediately after the execution of this contract the architect shall provide him (the contractor) ... with ... one copy certified ... of the Contract Documents; two further copies of the contract drawings; two copies of the unpriced Bills. *(Clause 5·2)*

IFC 84

Clause 1·1

There is a similar provision to JCT 80 Clause 2·1 above.

Clause 1·6

There is a similar provision to JCT 80 Clause 5·2 above. The same procedures are advised.

> The Architect ... shall provide ... one copy of the Contract Documents certified ... and two further copies of the contract drawings and the Specification/Schedules of Work/Contract Bills *(Clause 1·6)*

MW 80

Clause 1·1

This clause refers to the contract documents, but no specific requirements about their issue or custody are included.

Fig 1.1.1   Specimen AI issuing contract documents   For use with JCT 80

Issued by:
address:

Employer:
address:

Contractor:
address:

Works:
Situated at:

**Architect's
instruction**

Serial no:

Job reference:

Issue date:

Contract dated:

Under the terms of the above Contract, I/We issue the following instructions:

	Office use: Approx costs
	£ omit	£ add

ISSUE OF CONTRACT DOCUMENTS

We enclose:

.   one set of certified Contract Documents (refs.) of
     (date);
.   two sets of Contract Drawings;
.   two copies of the unpriced Bills of Quantities.

These documents are issued in accordance with clause 5.2 of
the contract.

[Add copy to: clerk of works]

To be signed by or for
the issuer named
above.   Signed _____

Amount of Contract Sum   £
± Approximate value of previous instructions   £ _____
                                                      £
± Approximate value of this instruction   £ _____
Approximate adjusted total   £

Distribution	☐ Employer	☐ Contractor	☐ Quantity Surveyor	☐ Services Engineer
	☐	☐ Nominated Sub-Contractors	☐ Structural Engineer	☐ File

© 1985 RIBA Publications Ltd

1.2 Issue of Further Drawings and Details

Volume 1
Action checklists
J2.1(70), K2.1(70)

The contractor will expect to be given drawings, instructions and any other information needed to carry out and complete the works according to the terms of the contract. The architect must provide such information within a reasonable time. Failure to do so may result in breach of contract by the employer.

As well as general explanatory information, the contractor may also request specific information. Where this is necessary, it should be issued according to the terms of the contract. Specific applications should be required, and blanket applications resisted.

If a request for further information requires an instruction varying work, the architect should assess the implications of delay and cost before issuing it.

The agreed procedure for issuing information should be followed and proper records kept. Further information should be issued under an Architect's Instruction, not by letter.

JCT 80

Clause 5·4
The contractor is entitled to two copies of any drawings or details necessary for carrying out the works. The cost of any additional copies requested by the contractor is chargeable, although the employer may agree that a reasonable number is provided free to assist the contractor's administration.

> As and when ... the Architect shall provide him (the Contractor) ... with 2 copies of such further drawings or details as are reasonably necessary ... *(Clause 5·4)*

IFC 84

Clause 1·7
There is a similar provision to JCT 80 Clause 5·4 above.

> The Architect shall provide him (the Contractor) with 2 copies of such further drawings or details as are reasonably necessary ... *(Clause 1·7)*

MW 80

Clause 1·2
There is a similar provision to JCT 80 Clause 5·4 above.

> The Architect shall issue any further information necessary ... *(Clause 1·2)*

Fig 1.2.1   **Specimen AI concerning payment for drawings**   For use with JCT 80

Issued by:
address:

Architect's instruction

Employer:
address:

Serial no:

Job reference:

Contractor:
address:

Issue date:

Contract dated:

Works:
Situated at:

Under the terms of the above Contract, I/We issue the following instructions:

| | Office use: Approx costs |
| | £ omit | £ add |

PAYMENT FOR DRAWINGS

This Instruction confirms the agreement reached at the
initial project meeting on (date) that you will be invoiced
monthly with the cost of all copies of drawings issued in
addition to those required under clause 5.2 of the contract.

Accounts should be settled within 30 days.

To be signed by or for
the issuer named
above.

Signed _____

Amount of Contract Sum	£
± Approximate value of previous instructions	£ _____
	£
± Approximate value of this instruction	£ _____
Approximate adjusted total	£

Distribution	☐ Employer	☐ Contractor	☐ Quantity Surveyor	☐ Services Engineer
	☐	☐ Nominated Sub-Contractors	☐ Structural Engineer	☐ File

© 1985 RIBA Publications Ltd

The complexity of modern documentation often results in inconsistencies, errors or omissions in and between documents.

Documents should be carefully checked for consistency before inviting tenders. Priced bills of quantities should be checked for errors before acceptance and, if errors are found in the tender, appropriate action should be taken, following the relevant NJCC Code of Procedure for selective tendering.

If an inconsistency, error or omission is found during the contract, the architect must issue a corrective instruction. This may constitute a variation, requiring an adjustment either way.

The quality and quantity of the work included in the contract sum are normally as described in the bills of quantities. To decide quality and quantity where no quantities are specified the documents are usually taken together, but the contract drawings prevail.

In any conflict between the printed conditions and the documents prepared for a particular job, it is common in the case of JCT contracts for the printed conditions to take precedence.

Volume 1
Action checklist J2.1 (70)
J6 Initial Project Meeting
Action checklist K2.1 (70)

JCT 80

Clause 2·2
Errors in the contract bills, or departures from the Standard Method of Measurement (SMM) method of preparation not specifically stated at the time of tendering, must be corrected by an Architect's Instruction and valued as a variation.

Clause 2·3
Discrepancies in or divergences between contract documents, any further drawings and details (including numbered documents where there are nominated sub-contractors) or any instructions must be corrected by an Architect's Instruction. The contractor is obliged to give the architect notice in writing immediately if he finds any discrepancies or divergences. The architect should carefully assess any cost implications, and advise the employer accordingly.

Clause 14·1
The quality and quantity of work covered in the contract sum is as set out in the bills of quantities. If there are no bills, then it is as described in the specification or schedules of work, or shown on the contract drawings. In the latter case, the contract drawings prevail.

> ... the departure or error or omission shall be corrected and such correction shall be treated as if it were a variation required by an instruction of the Architect ... *(Clause 2·2·2·2)*
>
> If the Contractor shall find any discrepancy in or divergence between ... the Contract Drawings, the Contract Bills, any instruction issued by the Architect ... any drawings or documents issued by the Architect ... the Numbered Documents ... the Architect shall issue instructions ... *(Clause 2·3)*

IFC 84

Clause 1·4

There is provision for correcting inconsistencies, errors or omissions, including NAM/T where applicable. There is no express requirement for the contractor to notify the architect in writing, but this is probably implied.

Clause 1·2

The quality and quantity of work covered in the contract sum is to be set out fully according to the contract documents used.

> The Architect shall issue instructions in regard to the correction of any inconsistency ... of any error in description ... of any error or omissions in the particulars (NAM/T) ... of any departure from the method of preparation of the Contract Bills ... *(Clause 1·4)*

MW 80

Clause 4·1

There is provision for correcting inconsistencies, but no express requirement for the contractor to notify the architect. Nor is there any express reference to the quality and quantity of work covered in the contract sum.

> Any inconsistency ... shall be corrected and any such correction ... shall be treated as a variation ... *(Clause 4·1)*

Issued by:
address:

Employer:
address:

Contractor:
address:

Works:
Situated at:

Architect's instruction

Serial no:

Job reference:

Issue date:

Contract dated:

Under the terms of the above Contract, I/We issue the following instructions:

	Office use: Approx costs	
	£ omit	£ add

CORRECTION TO BILLS OF QUANTITIES: Facing Brickwork

We confirm that there is an error in the Bills under (item). This should be corrected as follows:

    OMIT (item) on (page).

    SUBSTITUTE ....

This Instruction is issued in accordance with clause 2.3 of the contract.

[Add copy to: clerk of works]

To be signed by or for the issuer named above.

Signed _____

Amount of Contract Sum   £
± Approximate value of previous instructions   £ _____
  £
± Approximate value of this instruction   £ _____
Approximate adjusted total   £

Distribution	☐ Employer	☐ Contractor	☐ Quantity Surveyor	☐ Services Engineer
	☐	☐ Nominated Sub-Contractors	☐ Structural Engineer	☐ File

Volume 1
J6 Initial Project Meeting

It is important that a realistic contract period is stated in the tender documents, and this is a matter for the architect and employer to agree. The employer's requirements, site conditions, expenditure patterns and conditions in the industry at the time of tender will all be influential. Where early completion is essential or where other special circumstances apply, negotiation may be more appropriate than competition. For comparison, tenders might be sought both for the period fixed by the architect and for alternative periods.

The terms of the contract may require the contractor to submit an overall programme of work, and may require a particular type of programme.

A programme should never become a contract document, but it will give invaluable guidance about the contractor's intentions, what information he is likely to need, and how sub-contracted work and work carried out by persons engaged directly by the employer are to be integrated. It may also give a general indication of funding during the contract.

The architect should never approve a contractor's programme, for the organisation of working methods from possession to completion is the responsibility of the contractor. However, he is entitled to comment, and should not fail to raise with the contractor any matters of concern.

JCT 80

Clause 5·3·1·2
This clause may be deleted. If not, the contractor is required to provide a master programme as soon as possible after signing the contract. The programme is not a contract document. If extensions of time are given, the contractor must provide the architect with amended and revised copies within 14 days of such decisions. There is no definition of 'master programme' in the contract, and architects should state in the tender documents whether a particular type of programme is required, and whether it is to be produced before work starts.

> So soon as is possible ... the Contractor ... shall provide the Architect ... with 2 copies of his master programme ...
> *(Clause 5·3·1·2)*

IFC 84

There is no provision requiring a programme to be submitted. This would have to be written into the bills/schedules/specification as appropriate.

MW 80

As for IFC 84 above.

Fig 1.4.1   Specimen letter to contractor   For use with JCT 80
                   requiring a revised master programme

Following our Notification of Revision to the Completion Date
(no.) issued on (date), please send us two copies of your revised
Master Programme. We make this request in accordance with clause
5.3.1.2 of the contract, which requires you to supply this
information within 14 days.

Copies of the Notification have been issued to every nominated
sub-contractor in accordance with clause 25.3.5 of the contract,
and you should ensure the proper integration of their work in the
revised programme.

Copy to: employer, quantity surveyor, clerk of works

Custody of Contract Documents

The original contract documents are vital evidence in the event of a dispute and will also form the basis of the final account. They must be kept securely, treated as confidential, and used only for the purposes of the contract.

Volume 1
J7 Finalising the Contract

Although only one set of signed documents is needed to prove the existence of a contract, two are often prepared. One set is then held by the contractor and the other held by the employer. It is good practice for the architect to keep a third set in his office safe.

JCT 80

Clause 5·1
In the local authority edition the original contract documents are to be retained by the employer. In the private edition the original contract documents are to be retained by the architect or the quantity surveyor. Both the employer and the contractor are entitled to consult the original documents at all reasonable times.

IFC 84

Clause 1·6
The employer has custody of the contract documents. The contractor may inspect them at all reasonable times.

MW 80

There is no express reference to custody of the documents. The provisions of Clause 1·6 of IFC 84 could be adopted.

1.6 Use and Return of Contract Information

Contract information may only be used by the contractor for the purposes of the contract. If the architect wishes to ensure that information supplied is returned, he may issue an Architect's Instruction to this effect. This is particularly relevant in the case of Crown property, security establishments or highly sensitive commercial projects.

Where the contractor is supplied with copy negatives to make it easier for him to obtain tenders from domestic sub-contractors, these drawings may be endorsed as '*Copyright – to be used only for the purposes of this contract*' above the architect's name panel.

Unless otherwise agreed, or in the case of Crown property, the copyright of the works remains with the architect. Clearly, the risk of a breach of copyright is reduced if the architect asks for supplied information to be returned.

Where the contractor has paid for additional copies of drawings he may retain them, but they remain subject to the copyright conditions.

Volume 1
Action checklist F2.1 (70)
J6 Initial Project Meeting
Checklist Fig L8.1 Issuing
the Final Certificate

JCT 80

Clause 5·6
There is provision for the return of drawings at the request of the architect, but this applies only to documents which bear the name of the architect. In practice, the drawings etc of other consultants are usually also returned.

Clause 5·7
The reciprocal provisions of this clause ensure that confidentiality is maintained and that documents are used solely for the purposes of the contract.

> Upon final payment ... the Contractor shall ... return to him (the Architect) ... all drawings ... *(Clause 5·6)*

IFC 84

Clause 1·8
There is no provision for the return of documents, but limitations on their use are clearly stated. Return may be requested by letter.

MW 80

There is no express provision for returning documents or for limiting their use.

Fig 1.6.1   Specimen letter to contractor   For use with JCT 80
                   requesting the return of project documents

> Following the issue of the Final Certificate, would you please
> return all the drawings, details, descriptive schedules and other
> documents which we have issued in connection with the project?
>
> Please list the items, so that we can check them against issue.
>
> We make this request in accordance with clause 5.6 of the
> contract.

Volume 1
Action checklist
K2.1(70)

Once materials are brought to site (assuming that they conform to the standards of the contract), it should not be necessary to remove them. Only exceptional circumstances, such as a change in the programme of the works, adverse weather, damage to the works, security risks, labour difficulties etc, might warrant their removal.

Architects should carefully assess any requests for permission to remove materials, particularly those in short supply. If such requests persist, or if materials are removed from site without permission, the architect should investigate.

Although the contractor is responsible for the security of all materials on site, the architect should ensure that the employer's interests are properly protected. Once goods or materials have been paid for under an Interim Certificate, the architect should only allow their removal subject to stringent conditions. Where substantial items are involved, the employer should be advised before a decision is taken.

When drawing up the contract, the parties should clarify when the passing of property or ownership of goods and materials is to occur. Although there can be complications when there is retention of title, the general rule is that materials which are on site and have been paid for should stay there. They are owned by the employer.

JCT 80

Clause 16·1

Materials and goods delivered to the site may not be removed without the architect's written authorisation, but he cannot unreasonably withhold his consent. He may require the reasons for removal to be stated in writing.

The contractor is responsible for the security, storage and insurance of materials both on site and if subsequently removed from it, regardless of whether they have been included in an Interim Certificate, and irrespective of title.

Where unfixed materials and goods have been included under an Interim Certificate and paid for by the employer, Clause 16·1 states that they become the property of the employer. This will depend on whether the goods were owned by the contractor or sub-contractor in the first place, and the architect should check whether there is a retention of title clause in the contract under which the goods were supplied to the contractor or sub-contractor.

Clause 16·2

Materials and goods still unfixed and stored off site which have been included under an Interim Certificate and paid for by the employer become his property. They must not be moved from the premises where they are stored until required for the works. Architects should make sure that the employer has agreed to their inclusion and that the safeguards concerning identification set out in Clause 30·3 are complied with prior to inclusion in an Interim Certificate. It is wise to check this each time a further Interim Certificate is issued.

> Unfixed materials and goods ... shall not be removed ... unless the Architect has consented in writing ...
> *(Clause 16·1)*

IFC 84

Clause 1·10
There is a similar provision to JCT 80 Clause 16·1 above.

Clause 1·11
Provides for the payment of materials stored off site, but note that this contract does not set out obligations concerning storage. Architects would be wise to follow the requirements of JCT 80.

MW 80

There is no provision concerning the removal of materials, nor for paying for materials not on site.

Fig 1.7.1   Specimen AI agreeing to the removal of unfixed goods or materials from the site   For use with JCT 80

Issued by: address:		**Architect's instruction**
Employer: address:		Serial no: Job reference:
Contractor: address:		Issue date: Contract dated:
Works: Situated at:		

Under the terms of the above Contract, I/We issue the following instructions:

	Office use: Approx costs	
	£ omit	£ add

CONSENT·TO THE REMOVAL OF UNFIXED MATERIALS FROM THE SITE

We agree that you may remove (materials) from the site to allow modifications to be made to conform with drawing (no.). These modifications are to be carried out in the supplier's workshop, and you should ensure that the items are returned to the site promptly so as not to cause delay. This is all to be at no cost to the employer.

This Instruction is issued in accordance with clause 16.1.

[Add copy to: clerk of works]

To be signed by or for the issuer named above.

Signed _____

Amount of Contract Sum	£
± Approximate value of previous instructions	£ _____
	£
± Approximate value of this instruction	£ _____
Approximate adjusted total	£

Distribution   ☐ Employer   ☐ Contractor   ☐ Quantity Surveyor   ☐ Services Engineer

☐   ☐ Nominated Sub-Contractors   ☐ Structural Engineer   ☐ File

© 1985 RIBA Publications Ltd

'Watchpoints'

Published amendments

* Make sure that the form of contract incorporates any published amendments. Any special amendments required should be written into the actual form of contract.

Compatibility

* Check that the tender documents and the contract documents are compatible. Normally they will convey the same information, but last minute adjustments sometimes pass unnoticed. Contract documents should be precisely identified in the contract form. Note any definition of the term 'contract documents' in the form of contract being used.

Description of project

* Check that the works have been properly described in the contract form, that the physical extent of the site and the works has been clearly shown and that any special points concerning access or any restrictions to be imposed by the employer are included in the documents.

Completing the form

* Check that the form of contract has been properly completed, that decisions on option clauses are clearly shown, that specific information (eg in the Appendix) is complete and that the contract is signed or sealed before work commences.

Issuing the documents

* Issue copies of contract documents as required by the contract conditions. Arrange for a set to be kept for the employer. Issue a set to the contractor. Keep your own set in the office safe.

Consistency

* Check that the information in all documents issued is consistent, including 'numbered documents' if there are nominated or named sub-contractors. If any discrepancy or divergence is found, respond promptly and accurately with a corrective instruction.

Further information

* Issue further drawings or details as required. Attend to specific requests from the contractor promptly. He has a right to economic and expeditious completion in accordance with the contract and should not be held up by information being late. Use an Architect's Instruction for further information, quoting every drawing number and title, or document title, being issued.

Contractor's programme

* Study the contractor's programme and its implications for contract administration. Reference will be made to it at the initial project meeting and at subsequent architect's project meetings. In particular, note the dates for receipt of information required, nominated sub-contract periods and key delivery dates. Beware of accelerated programmes showing an intention to complete before the contract completion date. *Never approve the contractor's programme. Never interfere with the contractor's working methods*. Warn him if you see things which give you cause for concern.

Safekeeping
* Agree whether drawings are to be kept safe by the contractor and returned to you at the end of the job.

Removal of materials etc
* Establish at the outset that goods or materials brought to the site may not be removed from it without your written permission.

Note: items 7, 8, 9, 10 are relevant to the architect's initial project meeting (see Volume 1, J6).

Possession and Completion

2

References

JCT

Practice Notes
1:     Sectional Completion Supplement
16:    Extensions of Time and Liquidated Damages

IN/1: Date of Possession, Extension of Time, p4
IN/1: Appendix – Partial Possession

RIBA

'Practice'
Liquidated Damages (June 1985 p6)

The employer must give the contractor possession of the site on the date stated in the contract. In a project for new works this effectively means exclusive possession. Ownership of the site remains with the employer, who continues to be legally responsible. The contractor is not entitled to any rights or privileges in the ownership of the site unless otherwise agreed. The use and disposal of demolition debris, topsoil and excavated material should be clearly defined in the contract documents.

Unless the contract allows for deferment of possession, if the employer fails to give possession to the contractor on the date stated, he is in breach of contract. The contractor is entitled to clear possession of the site and uninterrupted access to it, subject only to any constraints written into the contract documents. If the site is not available on the date stated, then the employer and contractor must negotiate a new arrangement with amended dates for possession and completion. This could take the form of a supplemental agreement.

A definite date should be inserted whenever possible. Notifying the contractor that possession is to be within a certain number of weeks from the date the tender is accepted is not recommended, nor is the use of words such as 'date to be agreed'.

Problems may arise if the contractor fails to take possession of the site on the date stated, especially where sites are unsafe and there are dangerous structures. If the contractor does not take possession, the architect should immediately issue instructions requiring him to do so and should inform the employer. The insurance position should be checked and action taken as required.

Complications can arise where the employer wishes to remain in occupation of part of the works during the contract period. Thought should be given to the necessary arrangements, and some definite and precise description should be included in the documents at the time of tendering. A certain amount of give-and-take is necessary, and although this usually presents no real difficulty, it might be advisable to make certain that such an arrangement is properly incorporated into the text of the contract. The appropriate clause on possession (eg JCT 80 clause 23·1) could be qualified to make it clear that possession of the site '... subject to the proviso set out in item ... of the bills of quantities (item) ... shall be given to the contractor'.

Volume 1
Action checklist
H2.1 (70)

2.1 Possession

JCT 80

Clause 23·1

The contractor is required to begin the works on the date of possession. The employer must give possession on that day, unless Clause 23·1·1 in the Appendix applies and the employer wishes to defer possession. Such an action is a relevant event for which an extension of time may be given, and financial claims for disturbance may be valued under Clause 26·4. The contractor will need adequate time for pre-planning and mobilisation, and an initial project meeting is usually held to discuss arrangements. Formal handover of the site to the contractor is advisable, and the event should be recorded.

> On the Date of Possession, possession of the site shall be given to the Contractor ... *(Clause 23·1)*
>
> Where Clause 23·1·2 is stated in the Appendix to apply, the employer may defer the giving of possession ...
> *(Clause 23·1·2)*

IFC 84

Clause 2·1

There is similar provision to JCT 80 Clause 23·1. Similar action is recommended.

Clause 2·2

This clause provides for site possession to be deferred but, if it is to apply, this must be stated in the Appendix. It allows deferment for a period of up to six weeks, although a shorter period may be inserted in the Appendix. If the employer wishes to defer possession, an Architect's Instruction may be authorised. Such an action is an event for which an extension of time may be given, and financial claims for disturbance may be valid under Clause 4·11(a).

> Possession ... shall be given to the Contractor on the Date of Possession ... *(Clause 2·1)*
>
> ... the Employer may defer the giving of possession ...
> *(Clause 2·2)*

MW 80

Clause 2·1

Under this clause a date for site possession is to be inserted in the contract and the contractor may commence the works on that date. The employer will need to give the contractor a sufficient degree of possession to permit the execution of the works unimpeded by others. To avoid uncertainty, the architect should agree with the contractor a date for commencing the works.

> The Works may be commenced on ... and shall be completed by ... *(Clause 2·1)*

Fig 2.1.1   Specimen letter to contractor   For use with JCT 80
             confirming availability of site

Following the initial project meeting on (date), we confirm that
the site will be available for possession on (date), in
accordance with clause 23.1 of the contract.

Please telephone us to arrange a meeting on site to hand over the
keys.

Copy to: quantity surveyor, consultants, clerk of works

Issued by:
address:

Architect's instruction

Employer:
address:

Serial no:

Job reference:

Contractor:
address:

Issue date:

Contract dated:

Works:
Situated at:

Under the terms of the above Contract, I/We issue the following instructions:

	Office use: Approx costs	
	£ omit	£ add
DEFERRED POSSESSION OF SITE The employer has instructed us to inform you that possession of the site is deferred. This Instruction is issued in accordance with clause 23.1 of the contract. As soon as we have firm information we will let you know the revised date for possession. [Add copy to: clerk of works]		

To be signed by or for
the issuer named
above.   Signed _____

Amount of Contract Sum	£	
± Approximate value of previous instructions	£	_____
	£	
± Approximate value of this instruction	£	_____
Approximate adjusted total	£	

Distribution   ☐ Employer   ☐ Contractor   ☐ Quantity Surveyor   ☐ Services Engineer

☐   ☐ Nominated   ☐ Structural Engineer   ☐ File
                     Sub-Contractors

© 1985 RIBA Publications Ltd

Delayed Completion

The principal reason for including an extension of time provision is to protect the employer's right to claim liquidated damages in the event that he is the cause, in whole or part, of any delay.

Volume 1
Action checklists
K2.1 (70), L2.1 (70)

A definite date for completion should be inserted; there must be a precise date from which liquidated damages can run. The contract period can only be reduced with the agreement of the parties. The completion date may be revised (and this usually means an extension) subject to the terms of the contract.

The grounds on which an extension may be granted will be set out in the contract. Some are for matters wholly and solely the responsibility of the employer or his agents; others are for 'neutral' causes. Deletions in the printed text should not be made without careful thought about the consequences.

The administration of this provision is usually a matter for the architect alone. The authority is strictly limited by the contract conditions, and the procedural rules set out in the contract should be followed meticulously. It is important that the contractor notifies the architect of actual or likely delays promptly, so that measures may be taken to mitigate the consequences. The architect must respond quickly to every written notice of delay and assess what effect it may have upon the completion date. If the information provided by the contractor is not sufficient for the architect to deal with the claim, he should request more. In assessing concurrent delays, he must consider the effect of each cause separately.

The question of financial loss should not influence decisions about extensions of time. This should be considered separately.

The contractor is obliged to use his best endeavours to avoid delay or further delay. It is not generally considered that this imposes an obligation upon him to accelerate work at his own expense.

The employer must be notified of revisions to the completion date. It is advisable to draw his attention to the estimated financial implications at the same time.

JCT 80

Clause 25

The architect is required to consider any claim for an extension of time properly made by the contractor under Clause 25·2 and, if he thinks it is justified, to grant an extension of time, citing the relevant event and fixing a new completion date. The architect is not required to give any further information, but he should keep a record of any matters considered on the file for future reference.

The architect should not fail to give a decision within 12 weeks of receiving all the information necessary to consider the claim, assuming this is reasonably practicable; and on the same assumption, if less than 12 weeks remain to the contract completion date, the decision should be given within the time remaining.

Where the contractor's notice to the architect makes reference to a nominated sub-contractor, the contractor should send a copy of the written notice to the nominated sub-contractor concerned. If the completion date is being revised, the architect must notify all nominated sub-contractors.

During the 12 weeks following practical completion, the architect must review the contract completion date, taking into account any relevant matters, including delays due to the employer, but which have not been notified by the contractor.

It is also clear from Clause 25·3·2 that instructions issued in an overrun period, following the contractor's failure to complete on time, are authorised by the contract and can be covered by an extension of time.

The architect may confirm the date previously fixed, he may fix a date later than that previously fixed or, where work has been omitted, he may, subject to the restrictions in the contract, fix a completion date earlier than that previously fixed.

Under Clause 25·3·3 the architect may decide to review and finally fix the contract completion date once the stated contract completion date has been passed by the contractor, who has still not reached practical completion.

There is no power under the contract to reduce the contract period from that stated in the Appendix.

All decisions must be notified in writing. Under Clause 25·3·1 a written decision is required even where the architect decides that no change to the completion date is justified.

The Approximate Quantities version of JCT 80 provides for extensions of time in connection with work that could not have been foreseen at the time of tendering.

Clause 35·14

The contractor may apply to the architect in writing for permission to grant an extension of time to a nominated sub-contractor. He may not grant such an extension without the architect's written approval. Any extension of time is subject to the conditions of the NSC/4 or NSC/4a form of sub-contract.

If and whenever ... progress of the Works is being or is likely to be delayed, the Contractor shall forthwith give written notice ... *(Clause 25·2·1)*

... the Contractor shall, if practicable in such notice, or otherwise in writing as soon as possible ... give particulars of the expected effects ... estimate the extent, if any, of the expected delay ... *(Clause 25·2·2)*

The Contractor shall give such further written notices ... as may be reasonably necessary ... for keeping up-to-date the particulars and estimates ... *(Clause 25·2·3)*

... the Architect shall in writing ... give an extension of time ... as he then estimates to be fair and reasonable ... and shall, if reasonably practicable, ... fix such new Completion Date not later than 12 weeks from receipt of the notice and reasonably sufficient particulars ... *(Clause 25·3·1)*

After the Completion Date ... the Architect may, and not later than the expiry of 12 weeks after the date of Practical Completion, shall ... fix a Completion Date later than that previously fixed ... fix a completion date earlier than that previously fixed ... confirm to the Contractor the Completion Date previously fixed. *(Clause 25·3·3)*

The Architect shall notify ... to every Nominated Sub-contractor each decision ... *(Clause 25·3·5)*

The Architect shall operate the relevant provisions of Sub-contract NSC/4 ... upon receiving ... a request ... for his written consent to an extension ... *(Clause 35·14·2)*

IFC 84

Clause 2·3

The contractor is required to notify the cause of delay in writing. The architect must grant as soon as possible a fair and reasonable extension of time and confirm this in writing. He should ask the contractor for any further information needed to estimate the delay anticipated.

The clause refers only to extensions of time. There is no provision for making reductions where work has been omitted.

The architect has authority to grant extensions of time for reasons (which he must state) even after the contractor has failed to complete within the contract period. He has a discretionary power of review for up to 12 weeks following practical completion.

The contractor is nevertheless obliged to prevent delay by using his best endeavours.

> ... the contractor shall forthwith give written notice of the cause of the delay ... *(Clause 2·3)*
>
> ... if in the opinion of the Architect the completion ... is likely to be or has been delayed beyond the Date for Completion ... the Architect shall ... make in writing a fair and reasonable extension ... *(Clause 2·3)*
>
> At any time up to 12 weeks after the date of Practical Completion, the Architect may make an extension ... *(Clause 2·3)*

MW 80

Clause 2·2

The contractor is required to notify the architect if for reasons beyond his control the works will not be completed on time. The architect should grant a reasonable extension and confirm this in writing.

> If ... the Works will not be completed ... for reasons beyond the control of the Contractor, then the Contractor shall so notify the Architect ... *(Clause 2·2)*
>
> ... the Architect ... shall make, in writing, such extension ... as may be reasonable. *(Clause 2·2)*

Fig 2.2.1   Specimen letter to contractor   For use with JCT 80
requesting further information in connection with a notice
of delay

```
Thank you for your letter of (date) notifying a delay arising
from relevant events under clause 25.4.10.1 of the contract.

Please supply the following information, so that we can consider
this matter fully:

1    The programmed labour requirements for the period stated.

2    The numbers of joiners and assistant joiners employed on
     site during the critical period, and during the previous two
     months.

3    The rates paid to joiners and assistant joiners during the
     critical period and the previous two months.

4    What enquiries and advertisements for labour were made
     during the critical period and the previous two months.

You will appreciate that the clause you have referred to only
includes matters which you could not have reasonably foreseen
when tendering.



Copy to: quantity surveyor, clerk of works
```

Fig 2.2.2   Specimen letter to contractor   For use with JCT 80
rejecting an application for an extension of time

```
After careful consideration of your written notice of delay to
progress, and the further details which you sent in support of
your cited relevant event under clause 25.4.6 (ie late
information), we conclude that no revision to the completion date
is warranted.

The information which you requested was supplied within a
reasonable time of your specific application. The fact that you
are behind programme is obvious, but the cause appears to lie
elsewhere.



Copy to: quantity surveyor, clerk of works
```

Fig 2.2.3   **Specimen letter to contractor**   For use with JCT 80
agreeing an extension period for completing a nominated
sub-contract

> We refer to your letter of (date), which gives notice that
> nominated sub-contractor (name) has requested an extension to the
> sub-contract period.
>
> We have no objection to your granting this extension on the clear
> understanding that the extended sub-contract period can still be
> accommodated within your programme for the works.
>
> This consent is given in accordance with clause 35.14 of the
> contract.
>
>
> Copy to: quantity surveyor, clerk of works

Fig 2.2.4   **Specimen letter to employer**   For use with JCT 80
notifying a revision to the completion date

> We enclose a Notification of Revision to the Completion Date.
> This has been issued in accordance with clause 25.4 of the
> contract. We would remind you that the new completion date may
> affect your preparations for taking possession of the works.
>
> If you have any queries, please let us know.

The discovery of antiquities, particularly those of archaeological importance, may seriously delay the progress of building work. In some circumstances there might be statutory obligations, particularly those under the *Ancient Monuments and Archaeological Areas Act 1979*, which require compliance.

In an area where antiquarian finds are a strong possibility, the architect would be wise to warn the employer and give some guidance to the contractor before work starts.* The contract documents should anticipate the situation and stipulate suitable rules and procedures.

The question of ownership of smaller items and their safe-keeping pending examination and removal are matters sometimes expressly provided for in the standard building contracts. It is important that delicate objects are not damaged unnecessarily, and that there is minimum disturbance to the location of the find.

Volume 1
Action checklist K2.1 (70)

JCT 80

Clause 34
All fossils, antiquities and other objects of interest found on the site are the property of the employer. The contractor must avoid disturbing and damaging them, and must inform the architect or clerk of works of any finds.

The architect must issue instructions requiring the contractor to permit specialists to examine objects in situ. If direct loss and/or expense claims are valid, the amount ascertained is added to the contract sum. This is the only situation where the contract does not require written application by the contractor for direct loss. Claims for extensions of time may also arise, but in that case written notices of delay are required.

> ... the Contractor shall forthwith inform the Architect ...
> *(Clause 34·1)*
>
> The Architect shall issue instructions ... *(Clause 34·2)*

IFC 84

There are no express provisions concerning antiquities.

MW 80

There are no express provisions concerning antiquities.

---

* The Archaeologists and Developers Liaison Group (sponsored jointly by the Standing Committee of Archaeological Unit Managers, the British Property Federation, the Council for British Archaeology, the Historic Buildings and Monuments Commission, and the Institute of Field Archaeologists) encourages working practices through a voluntary code, and has a helpful code of practice for both archaeologists and developers.

Issued by:
address:

Architect's instruction

Employer:
address:

Serial no:

Job reference:

Contractor:
address:

Issue date:

Contract dated:

Works:
Situated at:

Under the terms of the above Contract, I/We issue the following instructions:

	Office use: Approx costs	
	£ omit	£ add

DISCOVERY OF OBJECTS ON SITE

Following your report of objects discovered on site, it is necessary to implement the actions set out in clause 34 of the contract, as follows:

1   Ensure that no work is carried out in the immediate area of the finds and that nothing is disturbed further.

2   Maintain a full-time security watch on site until further notice.

3   Provide secure and weathertight cover to the immediate area of the finds.

[Add copy to: clerk of works]

To be signed by or for
the issuer named
above.

Signed _____

Amount of Contract Sum	£	
± Approximate value of previous instructions	£	
	£	
± Approximate value of this instruction	£	
Approximate adjusted total	£	

Distribution   ☐ Employer   ☐ Contractor   ☐ Quantity Surveyor   ☐ Services Engineer

☐   ☐ Nominated Sub-Contractors   ☐ Structural Engineer   ☐ File

© 1985 RIBA Publications Ltd

If the contractor fails to complete on time, the employer is entitled to deduct liquidated damages, subject to the architect issuing a certificate to that effect. The employer must take care to comply with the provisions of the contract concerning notification and the time limits.

Volume 1
Action checklists
K2.1 (70), L2.1 (70)

If liquidated damages provisions are to operate, then a figure must be stated in the contract. It should be a genuine pre-estimate of the loss likely to be incurred, not a penalty sum. The loss does not have to be proved and, even if the employer suffers no loss in the event, the agreed figure is still recoverable.

Architects should explain to the employer the full implications of the provision and agree (and record) the figure to be inserted in the contract. If it cannot be accurately assessed it may be formula-based, taking into account capitalised interest, administrative costs, additional professional fees and exceptional costs. The figure inserted will be taken into account by the contractor when tendering.

Damages deducted immediately may have to be repaid if extensions of time are granted following practical completion.

A provision for bonus payments before the contract completion date is not normally included in standard forms and does not relate to liquidated damages for failure to complete on time.

JCT 80

Clause 24
The employer's right to deduct liquidated damages depends upon two things:
· that the architect has issued a Certificate of Non-completion, and
· that the employer has notified in writing his intention to claim liquidated damages.

The Certificate of Non-completion should be issued to the employer with a copy to the contractor. The right to claim liquidated damages ceases once the Final Certificate is issued, and the employer should be advised of the fact.

Clause 35·15
If a nominated sub-contractor fails to complete within the sub-contract period and the contractor notifies the architect of this, then the architect must issue a Certificate of Non-completion. However, he must check carefully that the extension of time provisions relating to the sub-contract have been properly applied. The certificate must be issued not later than 2 months after notification by the contractor, and this is a condition precedent to the contractor's claim for damages from the sub-contractor. The certificate is issued to the contractor, with a copy to the sub-contractor.

> ... the Architect shall issue a certificate ... *(Clause 24·1)*
>
> ... the Employer may deduct the same (liquidated damages) from any monies due ... to the Contractor under this contract ... *(Clause 24·2)*
>
> If any Nominated Sub-contractor fails to complete ... within the period specified ... the Architect shall so certify in writing to the Contractor ... *(Clause 35·15·1)*

IFC 84

Clause 2·6
A Certificate of Non-completion should be issued by the architect if the contractor fails to complete to time. The employer's right to deduct liquidated damages depends upon this and upon giving notice in writing to the contractor.

If after reviewing extensions of time a new completion date is fixed, the architect may need to issue a written cancellation of the certificate and a further certificate.

> If the Contractor fails to complete the Works by the Date for Completion ... the Architect shall issue a certificate ... *(Clause 2·6)*
>
> In the event of an extension ... the Architect shall issue a written cancellation of that certificate ... *(Clause 2·6)*
>
> Subject to the issue of a certificate ... the Employer may deduct (liquidated damages) from any monies due or to become due to the Contractor under this Contract ... *(Clause 2·7)*
>
> If ... the relevant certificate is cancelled the Employer shall pay or repay to the Contractor ... *(Clause 2.8)*

MW 80

Clause 2·3
There is no procedure for deducting liquidated damages. Nevertheless the architect would be wise to issue a formal certificate if the contractor fails to complete on time.

Despite the wording of the contract, it is almost certain that damages may be either paid to the employer or recovered by the employer by making a deduction from sums otherwise due to the contractor.

> ... then the Contractor shall pay to the Employer liquidated damages ... *(Clause 2·3)*

Fig 2.4.1   **Specimen letter to employer**   For use with JCT 80
concerning the implications of issuing a certificate of
non-completion

We have issued today a Certificate of Non-completion of the Works
in accordance with clause 24 of the contract. We draw your
attention to the implications of this event.

1   On the date of issue, liquidated and ascertained damages at
the rate of £ ..... per (time period) become due to you.
Damages will continue at this rate until the Certificate of
Practical Completion is issued.

2   These damages may be deducted at any time up to the issue of
the Final Certificate from monies due to the contractor, or
recovered from him as a debt.

3   Such deductions could begin immediately, but the contract
requires us to review extensions of time within 12 weeks of
practical completion, and this could mean an adjustment of
the contract period. In that case some repayment to the
contractor could become necessary.

It is essential that you notify the contractor in writing of your
intention to deduct liquidated damages before taking any action.

Copy to: quantity surveyor

Fig 2.4.2   **Specimen letter to employer**
cancelling a certificate of non-completion

There is no comparable provision in JCT 80, but it may be wise to
consider issuing a revised certificate of non-completion following
the review required by clause 25·3·3.

```
We have reviewed the extensions of time in accordance with clause
2.3 of the contract. The completion date has been revised to
(date), and it is necessary to cancel the Certificate of Non-
completion of (date).

This means that the contractor is not now liable for the payment
of liquidated damages for the period by which the contract has
been extended.



Copy to: quantity surveyor
```

Fig 2.4.3   **Specimen letter to contractor**
concerning the issue of a certificate of non-completion of
nominated sub-contract works

```
Thank you for your letter of (date) notifying us of the failure
of the nominated sub-contractor (name) to complete the nominated
sub-contract works within the sub-contract period.

We note your confirmation that there are no circumstances which
would warrant an extension of the sub-contract period, and that
this is accepted by the nominated sub-contractor.

We enclose a Certificate of Non-completion of this work issued
today. A copy has been sent to the nominated sub-contractor.



Copy to: quantity surveyor, consultant, clerk of works
```

Partial possession is not to be confused with sectional completion. It largely depends on the contractor's consent and may be subject to conditions.

Volume 1
Action checklists
K2.1 (70), L2.1 (70)

The architect should explain fully to the employer the risks and practicalities involved. Difficulties may arise in connection with safety, security, access, services and the progress of the remainder of the works. The employer must understand that he is responsible for insuring that part of the works which he has taken over. The architect must clearly identify the relevant part and fix the handover time precisely. Defects liability starts to run as soon as the relevant part is taken over, whether or not it is practically complete.

Where completion in phases or stages is a known requirement at the time of tendering, then this provision can be incorporated into the contract. It is better not to rely on clauses written into bills of quantities or a specification, because JCT contracts traditionally provide for the printed conditions to take priority. A suitable sectional completion supplement should be used to identify the sections and their respective completion dates, and this makes the recovery of liquidated damages, where sections are not completed on time, much more certain. Otherwise, liquidated damages may be linked to the completion date for the whole of the works.

Where the contract provides for partial possession and a pro rata reduction of liquidated damages according to the value of the relevant part, the way in which damages are set out in the Appendix should be consistent with the operation of the partial possession clause.

JCT 80

A Sectional Completion Supplement (JCT Practice Note 1) is available for use with JCT 80 either with quantities or with approximate quantities. It alters the First Recital by referring to phased completion, and introduces an Article 6, which sets out a Table of Changes necessary to modify the conditions. A special Appendix is included, which refers to three sections (more can be added if necessary). Any intention to use the Sectional Completion Supplement should be made known to tenderers. The adapted contract remains a single contract, and only one Final Certificate has to be issued.

Clause 18

With the consent of the contractor (and this must not be unreasonably withheld), the employer may take possession of any part of the works before contract completion. The architect must issue a written statement on behalf of the employer identifying precisely the relevant part and when the employer took possession of it. (It would be wise to include the time as well as the date.) Practical completion of the relevant part is then deemed to have occurred and the defects liability period starts to run. The employer is now responsible for insuring the relevant part. The amount included under the contract for liquidated damages is reduced pro rata.

This is an important matter which should be stated formally. If a Certificate of Partial Possession is used, care should be taken to see that it refers to the relevant part and the relevant date. The architect is not required to state the approximate value, although this information may be needed for any adjustment of insurance liabilities.

Clause 23·3

A reminder is given that insurance cover for the works is based on the assumption that the contractor has sole possession of them. If any part of the works is to be used by the employer before completion and is not subject to the partial possession proviso, the insurers must be informed at once.

> ... the Architect shall thereupon issue ... a written statement identifying the part or parts of the Works taken into possession and giving the date when the Employer took possession ... *(Clause 18·1)*
>
> ... the Contractor or the Employer shall notify the insurers under Clause 22A or Clause 22B or Clause 22C·2 to ·4 whichever may be applicable and obtain confirmation that such use or occupation will not prejudice the insurance ... *(Clause 23·3·2)*

IFC 84

A Sectional Completion Supplement (with guidance note) is available for use with this form of contract. It follows JCT 80.

Clause 2·9

A footnote refers to the action required if provision for partial possession is needed. This should be effected by a properly incorporated additional clause, as suggested in JCT Practice Note IN/1, the Appendix of which was revised in 1987:

2·11 If at any time or times before the date of issue by the Architect/the Contract Administrator of the certificate of Practical Completion the Employer wishes to take possession of any part or parts of the Works and the consent of the Contractor (which consent shall not be unreasonably withheld) has been obtained then, notwithstanding anything expressed or implied elsewhere in this Contract, the Employer may take possession thereof. The Architect/the Contract Administrator shall thereupon issue to the Contractor on behalf of the Employer a written statement identifying the part or parts of the Works taken into possession and giving the date when the Employer took possession (in clauses 2·11, 6·1·4 and 6·3C·1 referred to as 'the relevant part' and 'the relevant date' respectively); and

— for the purpose of clause 2·10 (*Defects liability*) and 4·3 (*Interim payment*) Practical Completion of the relevant part shall be deemed to have occurred and the defects liability period in respect of the relevant part shall be deemed to have commenced on the relevant date;

— when in the opinion of the Architect/the Contract Administrator any defects, shrinkages or other faults in the relevant part which he may have required to be made good under clause 2·10 shall have been made good he shall issue a certificate to that effect;

— as from the relevant date the obligation of the Contractor under clause 6·3A or of the Employer under clause 6·3B·1 or clause 6·3C·2 whichever is applicable, to insure shall terminate in respect of the relevant part but not further or otherwise; and where clause 6·3C applies the obligation of the Employer to insure under clause 6·3C·1 shall from the relevant date include the relevant part;

— in lieu of any sum to be paid or allowed by the Contractor under clause 2·7 (*Liquidated damages*) in respect of any period during which the Works may remain incomplete occurring after the relevant date there shall be paid or allowed such sum as bears the same ratio to the sum which would be paid or allowed apart from the provisions of clause 2·11 as the Contract Sum less the amount contained therein in respect of the said relevant part bears to the Contract Sum.

MW 80

There is no provision for partial possession, nor for sectional completion.

Fig 2.5.1   Specimen letter to employer   For use with JCT 80
              concerning the implications of partial possession

The contractor agrees that it will be possible for you to take
possession of the relevant part of the works, identified on the
attached drawing, on (date) in accordance with clause 18 of the
contract. There are a number of important implications:

1   The defects liability period on the relevant part begins on
      the relevant date.

2   Half of the retention percentage applying to the relevant
      part becomes due when certified.

3   The contractor ceases to be responsible for frost damage to
      the relevant part unless this is a result of damage which
      occurred before partial possession.

4   The contractor's liability for liquidated damages is reduced
      pro rata.

5   The insurance of the relevant part is your responsibility.
      We suggest that you discuss this with your insurance
      advisers now to ensure that appropriate cover takes effect
      from the relevant date.

Please let us know if you need any further explanation of the
implications of partial possession and the associated procedures.

Copy to: quantity surveyor

Practical completion means that the whole of the work to be done under the contract is complete in all respects, except for any latent defects. The architect should only certify practical completion when he considers that this stage has been reached. Certificates which are qualified by an attached list of outstanding or unfinished items are not satisfactory, and contracts make no provision for such qualification. Furthermore, the omission of certain items can make some of the contract conditions inoperable. However, if for some good reason such a certificate has to be issued, then the schedule of items not included should be referred to on the face of the certificate. Architects who have entered into collateral agreements with third parties should be particularly careful in these circumstances and should obtain an indemnity from any employer who is pressing for practical completion to be certified.

The architect alone has to decide whether a state of practical completion has been achieved. His decision must not be influenced by pressure from either the contractor or the employer. However, he is obliged to issue a certificate when practical completion has been achieved; failure to do so constitutes a breach of contract by the employer through his agent, the architect.

Once a Certificate of Practical Completion has been issued, it cannot be withdrawn (although its issue may be reviewed by an arbitrator).

The issue of the certificate starts the defects liability period and releases the contractor from any obligation to insure the works. It is important that the employer understands the significance of practical completion and arranges for insurance of the works to begin as soon as the certificate is issued.

Although 'snagging' (listing small defects for making good after practical completion) is widely practised in the industry, it is rarely made a contract provision. It is not the responsibility of the architect to provide the contractor with lists of items to be made good before practical completion. The contractor is responsible for making certain that the works are complete before asking the architect to certify practical completion.

There is only one certificate of practical completion for 'the works' (or for each section of the works where a Sectional Completion Supplement is used). However, it may be a contractual obligation in some cases also to certify separately the practical completion of sub-contract works. The procedures laid down in the contract clauses should be closely followed.

Notify the client in good time that practical completion is approaching, and in particular draw attention to his responsibility for insurance. Ensure that the architect's as-built drawings and maintenance manual (in accordance with the terms of the agreement) are initiated in good time, including liaison with the structural engineer and other consultants, manufacturers etc, so that they are ready for handover at the practical completion inspection.

JCT 80

Clause 17

The architect is required to issue a Certificate of Practical Completion when he considers that the works have reached this stage. The effective date should be stated in the certificate.

The issue of the certificate starts the defects liability period, ends the contractor's responsibility for insuring the works, and enables part of the retention to be released. The architect should write to the employer to advise him about the implications of issuing the certificate.

Clause 35·16

The architect is required to certify practical completion in respect of each nominated sub-contractor's work. The main contractor should notify the architect of the completion of sub-contract works, adding his own observations about the the sub-contractor's work. Certification is a matter for the architect alone. The certificate is issued to the main contractor, with a copy to the nominated sub-contractor.

> When in the opinion of the Architect ... Practical Completion ... is achieved, he shall forthwith issue a certificate ... *(Clause 17·1)*
>
> When in the opinion of the Architect Practical Completion of the Works executed by a Nominated Sub-contractor is achieved, he shall forthwith issue a certificate ... *(Clause 35·16)*

IFC 84

Clause 2·9

The provision is similar to that in JCT 80 Clause 17 above.

> When in the opinion of the Architect ... he shall forthwith issue a certificate ... *(Clause 2·9)*

MW 80

Clause 2·4

The architect is required simply to certify practical completion, and to name the date it became effective.

> The Architect shall certify the date ... *(Clause 2·4)*

We are about to issue the Certificate of Practical Completion in accordance with clause 17 of the contract. There are a number of important implications:

1   The contractor's liability to pay liquidiated damages ceases.

2   The defects liability period begins.

3   The contractor ceases to be responsible for frost damage which occurs subsequently.

4   The period of final measurement begins, and half of the retention percentage is released.

5   Insurance of the works becomes your responsibility. We suggest that you discuss this with your insurance advisers now to ensure that appropriate cover takes effect from the date of the certificate.

6   We review the contract completion date as directed by Clause 25.3.3 of the contract.

Please let us know if you need any further information about the procedures or implications of practical completion.

Copy to: quantity surveyor

The defects liability provisions entitle the contractor, for a certain period, to return to site to make good his own defects. Subject to the contract terms, this does not exclude or limit the employer's right in common law to recover damages for consequential losses suffered as a result of defective work.

The contractor's liability is limited to making good defects arising from materials or workmanship which are not in accordance with the contract and which appear during the defects liability period, or from frost damage which occurs before practical completion. Unless the contract specifically provides for it, the contractor is not responsible for maintenance during these periods.

The architect is required to issue a schedule of defects within a stated time after the end of the defects liability period and the contractor is required to make them good within a reasonable time from receiving this schedule, and at his own expense. If it is impossible to do this without causing the employer serious disruption, it may be agreed to extend the period for making good.

Alternatively, other arrangements for making good the defects (with an appropriate financial adjustment) may be agreed. In these circumstances it is still necessary to prepare the schedule so as to inform the contractor of the extent of the defects. This should be accompanied by an Architect's Instruction which clearly states the employer's decision that the defects will not be made good under the contract. The amount of the 'appropriate deduction' to be made in the adjustment is a matter for the quantity surveyor.

In an emergency, the architect may require defects to be made good during the defects liability period.

Where there are defects and the contractor is under an obligation to rectify them, the architect is required to certify when they have been made good; this is a requirement for final payment to be made.

There should be only one defects liability period for a building contract and it should be long enough to establish the adequate performance of service installations, etc.

Where landscape work is carried out under a separate contract, or under supplemental conditions incorporated in a building contract, it is usual to find a provision to cover the failure of plants (pre-practical completion) and the maintenance of trees, shrubs, grass etc post-practical completion.

Volume 1
Action checklist L2.1 (70)
L4 Handover
L7 Final Inspection

JCT 80

Clause 17·2

The schedule of defects which must be issued within 14 days of the end of the defects liability period may either be listed as an Architect's Instruction or attached to one, dated and referenced.

The defects must be clearly identified and located, but it is not generally necessary to specify how they are to be made good. The contractor's obligation is limited to meeting the requirements of the contract documents. Any remedial action specified in excess of those requirements would be *ultra vires* and would require the agreement of the parties and appropriate financial arrangements.

After issuing the schedule, the architect is not empowered under the contract to issue further instructions for making good additional defects. Therefore he should take great care to ensure that this schedule is complete. If the employer does not wish the defects to be made good by the contractor, he may authorise the architect to instruct the contractor accordingly, and an appropriate deduction is made from the contract sum.

Clause 17·3

The architect may issue instructions for making good defects during the defects liability period, and the contractor is required to do so within a reasonable time. In the interests of both the employer and the contractor, these instructions should be restricted to matters which cannot reasonably be deferred until the end of the period.

Clause 17·4

On the completion of making good defects described in instructions issued under Clause 17·3 and scheduled under Clause 17·2, the architect is required to inspect the work. If satisfied, he should issue a Certificate of Completion of Making Good Defects. The outstanding retention is released under an architect's certificate.

Clause 35·18

Defects in a nominated sub-contractor's work must be made good by the nominated sub-contractor before receiving final payment. The normal procedures for issuing a schedule of defects and a Certificate of Completion of Making Good Defects should be followed, although there is no formal defects liability period or time limit for the issue of lists of defects. Obviously the main contractor, whose opinions of the sub-contract works were included at practical completion, will be consulted. Clause 35·17·1 expressly refers to the opinion of the architect *and* the contractor.

Early final payment of nominated sub-contractors is only required where Agreement NSC/2 or NSC/2a is in operation. Following final payment, if further defects appear before the Final Certificate is issued, the nominated sub-contractor is still obliged to rectify them. If he fails to return to site, the architect may nominate a substitute sub-contractor to carry out this work, the cost of which should in theory be recoverable from the defaulting sub-contractor under the terms of NSC/2. But if this is not possible, in spite of the employer taking all reasonable steps to recover and the main contractor agreeing the price to be charged by the substitute sub-contractor, then the main contractor is liable.

The contractor cannot be held responsible for defects arising from the sub-contractor's design, selection of materials or failure to meet performance specification requirements. Although the main contractor has a duty to supervise the work of sub-contractors and is liable for the materials and workmanship of nominated sub-contractors, he is not obliged to put right any defects himself.

> Any defects, shrinkages or other faults ... shall be specified by the Architect in a schedule of defects ... *(Clause 17·2)*
>
> ... the Architect may ... issue instructions requiring any defect, shrinkage or other fault ... to be made good ... *(Clause 17·3)*
>
> When ... defects, shrinkages or other faults ... shall have been made good he (the Architect) shall issue a certificate ... *(Clause 17·4)*
>
> ... unless the Architect, with the consent of the Employer, shall otherwise instruct ... then an appropriate deduction in respect of any defects, shrinkages or other faults not made good shall be made from the Contract Sum. *(Clause 17·2)*
>
> ... if the original Sub-contractor fails to notify any defect, shrinkage or other fault ... the Architect shall ... issue an instruction nominating a person ("the substituted Sub-contractor") ... *(Clause 35·18·1)*

IFC 84

Clause 2·10

The architect is required to notify the contractor of defects, shrinkages or other faults not later than 14 days after the end of the defects liability period. These should be made good at no cost to the employer within a reasonable time. The architect is required to issue a certificate when this has been satisfactorily done.

It is recommended that notification should take the form of a schedule, preferably attached to an Architect's Instruction, although this is not required by the contract provision.

> Any defects, shrinkages or other faults ... notified by the Architect ... shall be made good by the Contractor ... *(Clause 2·10)*
>
> The Architect shall, when in his opinion ... obligations under Clause 2·10 have been discharged, issue a certificate ... *(Clause 2·10)*

MW 80

Clause 2·5

The contractor is obliged is to make good defects, excessive shrinkage and other similar faults which appear within a specified time of practical completion. The architect should certify when this has been done satisfactorily.

It is recommended that defects are listed in writing or in a schedule, preferably attached to an Architect's Instruction, although this is not a requirement under the contract.

> Any defects, excessive shrinkages or other faults ... shall be made good by the Contractor ... *(Clause 2·5)*
>
> The Architect shall certify ... when ... the Contractor's obligations ... have been discharged. *(Clause 2·5)*

'Watchpoints'

Note: all these items are relevant to the architect's regular progress meetings.

Site possession

* The whole site should be available for the contractor to take possession on the date stated. If there are likely to be problems, advise the employer.

Deferred possession

* If possession is deferred, the required timing and procedures must be carefully followed. Obtain written authority from the employer before taking any action and his agreement to any repercussions on costs.

Notice of delay

* Respond promptly if delays are notified. Check the effect on progress and consider what remedial action is possible. Make reasonable requests to the contractor for supporting information. Watch over the employer's interests if he is the cause of delay.

Granting extensions

* Keep to the events or causes set out in the particular contract – you have no power to grant extensions for other reasons. Take the relevant circumstances into account, and relate the delay to the contract completion date. Identify the relevant events considered, but do not allocate specific periods of time against each. Be as fair as possible in the particular circumstances and make sure that you follow the timing and procedures set out in the contract. Always respond in writing to an application, even if the answer is negative.

The contract period

* On completion, if directed or authorised by the contract, review extensions of time previously granted, or which should now be considered. Confirm decisions in writing, even if there is no change. Send copies as required by the contract.

Partial possession

* Advise the employer of the implications of partial possession. Obtain the contractor's consent and identify precisely in writing the relevant part and the time of handover.

Non-completion

* Issue the Certificate of Non-completion immediately after the completion date stated in the contract. Advise the employer that it can be cancelled if the contract period is extended.

Practical completion

* Only issue a Certificate of Practical Completion when you are of the opinion that the works are complete. Resist requests to issue a qualified or conditional certificate. If necessary, seek an indemnity from the employer, particularly if you have entered into third party collateral agreements.

Defects liability

* Establish one defects liability period to cover all work. Make sure that a schedule of defects is ready at the end of the defects liability period. When defects have been made good and you are completely satisfied, issue a Certificate of Completion of Making Good Defects. If in lieu there is to be a cash adjustment, make sure that you get the employer's authorisation in writing.

Control of the Works 3

continued

References

JCT

Practice Notes

9: Domestic Sub-contractors
10: Nomination of Sub-contractors
11: Employer/Nominated Sub-contractor Agreements
13: Re-nomination
14: Variations and Provisional Sum Work
15: Nominated Suppliers

Standard Forms

of Nominated Sub-contract Tender and Agreement (NSC/1, NSC/1a)
of Employer/Nominated Sub-contract Agreement (NSC/2, NSC/2a)
of Nomination of Sub-contractor (NSC/3, NSC/3a)
of Nominated Sub-contract (NSC/4, NSC/4a)
of Tender by Nominated Supplier (TNS/1) (optional)
Warranty by a Nominated Supplier (TNS/2) (optional)

Practice Notes

IN/1: Variations, Testing, Setting Out, p5
IN/1: Naming a Sub-contractor p7

Form of Tender and Agreement (NAM/T)
Sub-contract Conditions for Named Sub-contractors (NAM/SC)

NJCC

Procedure Notes

4: Contracts with substantial building services content
14: Sub-contracts involving preparation of drawings and off-site fabrication work by the sub-contractor
15: Commissioning and testing
16: Record drawings and operating and maintenance instructions
17: Set off and adjudication procedures under sub-contract

RIBA

RIBA/CASEC

Form of Employer/Specialist Agreement (ESA/1)

'Practice'

IFC Preliminaries – listing of sub-contractors (February 1985, p7)
Sub-contract Warranties (June 1985 p4)
Architect's inspection duties under *Architect's Appointment* and the Standard Form of Building Contract (September 1987 p1)
Specialist Sub-contractors' retention money (April 1988 p1)

'Watchpoints'

3.1 Assignment

Assignment in connection with building contracts is not normally a matter which involves the architect directly – it is a matter for the parties to the contract.

Assignment is the means by which contractual interests may be transferred. This may be by way of security for a loan or where a party is disposing of the whole or part of his business. In a contract of a personal nature it may be because of the death or incapacity of one of the parties. Sometimes the contractor has a business arrangement whereby monies can be paid direct to some other party. (In other words, he wishes to assign the rights to payments due under the contract whilst retaining the contractual obligations.) Contracts often expressly prohibit unilateral attempts at assignment.

An agreement to assign can be written into a contract or into a collateral warranty of the sort often presented to architects. Any such agreement should be carefully considered before signature.

Where all parties have agreed that the original contractor should be replaced by another, a new contract is drawn up to complete the works. This may substitute for the original contract or be read in conjunction with it. The terms will not necessarily be those of the original contract. This is known as a 'novation' agreement.

JCT 80

Clause 19·1
Either party needs the written consent of the other before this contract may be assigned (the implication being that this applies to benefits as well as burdens).

Clause 19·1·2
Introduced as an option under Amendment 4:1987. Where it is stated in the Appendix to apply, this clause allows the employer to assign a right of action in the event of transfer of a freehold or leasehold interest in the works. It is limited to post-practical completion, and only in respect of matters arising out of the building contract other than those which are already the subject of an enforceable agreement between the parties.

IFC 84

Clause 3·1
There is a similar provision to Clause 19·1·1 of JCT 80.

MW 80

Clause 3·1
There is a similar provision to Clause 19·1·1 of JCT 80.

The general rule is that the contractor carries out the work which he has undertaken to do. There is no implied right to sub-contract work. Where the architect suspects that unauthorised sub-contracting is likely to occur, a general warning letter may be appropriate.

Volume 1
Action checklists
C2.1 (70), D2.1 (70),
E2.1 (70), F2.1 (70),
G2.1 (70), H2.1 (70)

Most building contracts accept the custom of sub-contracting, subject to the terms of the contract in question. (It should be noted here that the JCT standard form, JCT 80, refers to this practice as 'sub-letting', although the sub-lessors are referred to as 'sub-contractors'. For the sake of consistency, this book refers to sub-contracting and sub-contractors throughout.)

Sub-contracting is clearly inappropriate where the particular skills or expertise of a party is being relied upon or where the contract is of a personal nature. However if the contractor requests permission to sub-contract, it would be wise to ask to be given names of referees and the locations of work carried out by the sub-contractors proposed.

If there is nothing to the contrary in the contract, the original party remains responsible for the work undertaken and for any failure to carry out that work properly and fully.

The sub-contractor is not bound by the terms of the main contract unless they are also part of the sub-contract. So unless the terms of the main contract stipulate the use of a particular form of sub-contract, this is for the contractor and sub-contractor to agree.

Provided that there is no collateral agreement, there is no privity of contract between employer and sub-contractor. ('Privity' means that only the parties to the contract can acquire rights and obligations under it.) But whenever there is reliance upon the specialist skill of a sub-contractor in matters of design, performance or selection of materials – all matters normally outside the scope of building contracts of a 'work and materials' type – then a collateral agreement is in the employer's interests.

Some useful terminology

The following unofficial definitions may be helpful to users of JCT forms of contract:

Approved sub-contractor:
domestic sub-contractor approved by the architect.

Listed person as sub-contractor:
domestic sub-contractor selected by the contractor from a list prepared by the architect.

Named person as sub-contractor:
domestic sub-contractor chosen by the architect.

Nominated sub-contractor:
not a domestic sub-contractor. Appointment is as directed by the architect and funded by a prime cost sum.

JCT 80

Clause 19·2

The contractor must not sub-contract any portion of the work without the written consent of the architect. This may not be unreasonably withheld to the prejudice of the contractor. Where it is reasonably withheld, the contractor will not be entitled to loss and expense.

It would be wise to ask the contractor to request consent in good time. Whilst the clause seems to refer only to the *principle* of sub-contracting, it seems reasonable that the architect should be given details of the persons concerned. In the absence of their names, it would be difficult for the architect to be satisfied that the employer's interests were protected.

There is no requirement for domestic sub-contracts to be on any particular form (although the Building Employers Confederation have published an appropriate form, DOM/1). Clause 19·4 (see JCT 80 Amendment 1:1984) makes it a condition that terms relating to the employer's ownership of unfixed goods and materials are included in any domestic sub-contract.

> The contractor shall not without the written consent of the Architect ... sub-let any portion of the works ...
> *(Clause 19·2)*

IFC 84

Clause 3·2

There is a similar provision to Clause 19·2 of JCT 80. The obligation for the contractor to include terms relating to determination and property in goods and materials in a sub-contract is printed in the text of the main contract.

> The Contractor shall not sub-contract ... without the written consent of the Architect ... *(Clause 3·2)*

MW 80

Clause 3·2

The contractor must not sub-contract any portion of the work without the written consent of the architect. The architect's consent may not be unreasonably withheld to the prejudice of the contractor.

> The Contractor shall not sub-contract ... without the written consent of the Architect ... *(Clause 3·2)*

Fig 3.2.1   **Specimen letter to contractor**   For use with JCT 80
concerning unauthorised sub-contracting

We understand that you have sub-contracted work to (name) without
our written permission. This is in contravention of clause 19.2
of the contract and must cease immediately.

No further sub-contracting should proceed without our written
approval of the proposed sub-contractor, in accordance with the
provisions of the contract.

Copy to: quantity surveyor, clerk of works

Issued by:
address:

Employer:
address:

Contractor:
address:

Works:
Situated at:

Architect's instruction

Serial no:

Job reference:

Issue date:

Contract dated:

Under the terms of the above Contract, I/We issue the following instructions:

	Office use: Approx costs	
	£ omit	£ add

CONSENT TO SUB-CONTRACTING

We consent to the sub-contracting of the work described in your letter (ref.) of (date), namely:

1   External painting to: (name)

2   Paving to: (name)

3   Precast concrete to: (name)

This Instruction is issued in accordance with clause 19.2 of the contract.

[Add copy to clerk of works]

To be signed by or for
the issuer named
above.   Signed _____

Amount of Contract Sum	£	
± Approximate value of previous instructions	£	_____
	£	
± Approximate value of this instruction	£	_____
Approximate adjusted total	£	

Distribution   ☐ Employer   ☐ Contractor   ☐ Quantity Surveyor   ☐ Services Engineer

☐   ☐ Nominated Sub-Contractors   ☐ Structural Engineer   ☐ File

© 1985 RIBA Publications Ltd

The term 'listed persons' (under the margin heading *Sub-letting – List in Contract Bills etc.*) is confined to JCT 80.

This is a long-established method of indicating in the tender documents which work is to be sub-contracted to a domestic sub-contractor. The contractor's choice is limited to a list of firms acceptable to the architect. In this way nomination is avoided – which means that the contractor is wholly responsible for the performance of the sub-contractor. If the selected firm is subsequently unable or unwilling to enter into a sub-contract then, subject to the main contract conditions, the problem rests with the contractor.

Although this way of specifying sub-contractors is formally recognised in JCT 80 only, it can easily be adapted for use in other contexts. It can be used with MW 80, and the National Building Specification suggests how it can be used with IFC 84.

Listed sub-contractors often complain about the so-called 'Dutch auction' to which they can be subjected by a main contractor after he has tendered successfully. Architects wishing to mitigate this situation might require the contractor to identify which firm he intends to sub-contract to if his tender is accepted.

Volume 1
Action checklists
C2.1 (70), D2.1 (70),
E2.1 (70), F2.1 (70),
G2.1 (70), H2.1 (70)

JCT 80

Clause 19·3

A list of not less than three persons able and willing to undertake certain sub-contract work is to be included in or annexed to the bills/specification. The work must be described in sufficient detail for the contractor to obtain prices. He is free to choose any name from the list, and the chosen firm will have the status of a domestic sub-contractor.

The list must contain not less than three valid names at the time the main contractor wishes to execute the sub-contract. A mechanism is provided for either the contractor or the employer to top up the list as necessary. It might be sensible to compile an initial list of, say, five names to reduce the risk of this becoming necessary. The contractor is bound by the figure included in his tender.

If it proves impossible to find other names to bring the list up to the minimum required, the contractor may sub-contract. It might also be sensible to ask the contractor to identify which of the firms listed he proposes using when he submits his tender. However, JCT 80 does not require this.

> Where the Contract Bills provide ... certain work ... must be carried out by persons named in a list ... The list ... must comprise not less than three persons. Either the Employer ... or the Contractor shall be entitled with the consent of the other ... to add additional persons ... *(Clause 19·3)*

3.3 'Listed Persons' as Sub-contractors

IFC 84

There is no provision for listed persons as sub-contractors in the conditions.

MW 80

There is no provision for listed persons as sub-contractors in the conditions.

Fig 3.3.1

Specimen letter to contractor proposing an addition to the list of domestic sub-contractors

For use with JCT 80

```
      Please refer to (item) on (page) of the Bills of Quantities,
      where sub-contractors for (type of work) are listed.

      In accordance with clause 19.3 of the contract, we have been
      instructed by the employer to propose that (name) should be added
      to the list. We will be pleased to receive your consent to this
      addition.

      This will be at no extra cost to the employer.



      Copy to: employer, quantity surveyor, consultant
```

Fig 3.3.2

Specimen letter to contractor consenting to an addition to the list of domestic sub-contractors

For use with JCT 80

```
      We refer to your letter of (date) in which you propose the
      addition of (name) to the list of domestic sub-contractors for
      (type of work).

      We confirm the consent of the employer to this proposal, which is
      given in accordance with clause 19.3 of the contract.

      This will be at no extra cost to the employer.



      Copy to: employer, quantity surveyor, consultants
```

Fig 3.3.3   Specimen AI concerning additions to the list of domestic sub-contractors   For use with JCT 80

Issued by:
address:

Architect's instruction

Employer:
address:

Serial no:

Job reference:

Contractor:
address:

Issue date:

Contract dated:

Works:
Situated at:

Under the terms of the above Contract, I/We issue the following instructions:

	Office use: Approx costs	
ADDITIONS TO LIST OF DOMESTIC SUB-CONTRACTORS	£ omit	£ add

ADDITIONS TO LIST OF DOMESTIC SUB-CONTRACTORS

Add the following names to the list of domestic sub-contractors for wall tiling under (item) on (page) of the Bills of Quantities:

     (name)

     (name)

This Instruction is issued in accordance with clause 19.3 of the contract.

The list now contains the names of three firms who are understood to be able and willing to carry out this work.

[Add copy to clerk of works]

To be signed by or for the issuer named above.

Signed _____

	£	
Amount of Contract Sum	£	
± Approximate value of previous instructions	£	_____
	£	
± Approximate value of this instruction	£	_____
Approximate adjusted total	£	

Distribution   ☐ Employer   ☐ Contractor   ☐ Quantity Surveyor   ☐ Services Engineer

☐   ☐ Nominated Sub-Contractors   ☐ Structural Engineer   ☐ File

© 1985 RIBA Publications Ltd

3.4 'Named Persons' as Sub-contractors

In JCT documents the term 'named person as sub-contractor' is confined to IFC 84.

For a long time it has been common practice, particularly with smaller jobs, to name one firm in tender documents, and to require the contractor to use that firm for certain parts of the works. The contractor remains wholly liable for their performance and is bound by whatever figure he included in his tender.

However, difficulties can arise if the named firm is subsequently unable or unwilling to enter into a sub-contract and the contract conditions do not include any mechanism for substituting a new name. The employer could then find himself in difficulties.

Where the contract does not expressly provide for naming, it might be more appropriate to include a restricted list of names from which the contractor can choose.

Volume 1
Action checklists
C2.1 (70), D2.1 (70),
E2.1 (70), F2.1 (70),
G2.1 (70), H2.1 (70)

JCT 80

There is no provision for named persons as sub-contractors.

IFC 84

Clause 3·3
There are two procedures for naming:

Procedure (1)
The name of the person selected will be included in the bills/specification/schedules, with a full description of the work and particulars of tender. Form NAM/T with Sections I and II completed, together with supporting 'numbered documents' and 'priced documents', must also be provided (see First Recital).

Procedure (2)
A provisional sum will be included in the bills/specification/schedules. Form NAM/T with Sections I and II completed, together with 'numbered documents' and 'priced documents', must be provided when the Architect's Instruction concerning the expenditure of a provisional sum is issued.

In Procedure (1) the contractor has no right of objection; he will automatically enter into the sub-contract within 21 days of entering into the main contract. All particulars of NAM/T must be correct; architects should make sure that the contractor and the named person are in complete agreement when the main contract is signed otherwise further instructions may need to be issued, and these could have implications in terms of time and money.

In Procedure (2) the contractor has a right of reasonable objection; otherwise he must enter into a sub-contract within 14 days of the issue of the Architect's Instruction. A sustainable objection might require the architect to issue further instructions.

The use of the JCT NAM/T Form of Tender and Agreement is obligatory. Section III incorporates sub-contract conditions NAM/SC by reference. The main contractor is expressly not

Fig 3.4.1   Naming: Procedure (1) (Clause 3·3·1)

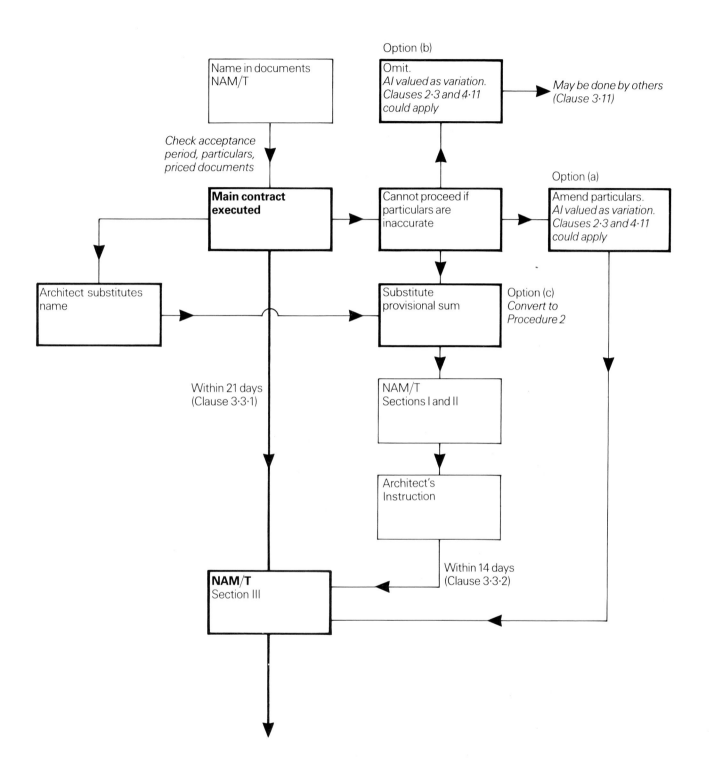

responsible for the design work, selection of materials, or the meeting of performance specifications by the named person. Whenever design work is undertaken by named persons, insist that the RIBA/CASEC form ESA/1, Employer/Specialist Agreement, is used.

If the named person's employment is determined, the architect must issue further instructions as set out in the contract. The options are:
(a)   to name another person;
(b)   to instruct the main contractor to make his own arrangements;
(c)   to omit the remaining work, which may be completed under arrangements made directly by the employer.

If it is necessary to have any defective work by the defaulting named person rectified, make sure that this is accounted separately.

There is no provision in IFC 84 allowing a main contractor to tender for work which is stated to be reserved for a named person. If this is required, the architect could substitute a provisional sum in place of the name included and issue instructions for its expenditure.

Where it is stated ... that work ... is to be executed by a named person ... the Contractor shall not later than 21 days ... enter into a sub-contract ... using Section III of ... NAM/T referred to in the 1st Recital. *(Clause 3·3·1)*

If the Contractor is unable ... he shall immediately inform the Architect ... the Architect shall issue an instruction. *(Clause 3·3·1)*

The Contractor shall notify the Architect of the date when he has entered into the sub-contract ... *(Clause 3·3·1)*

In an instruction as to the expenditure of a provisional sum ... the Architect may require work to be executed by a named person ... *(Clause 3·3·2)*

Unless the Contractor shall have made reasonable objection ... within 14 days ... he shall enter into a sub-contract ... using Section III of ... NAM/T ... *(Clause 3·3·2)*

The Contractor shall advise the Architect ... of any events which are likely to lead to any determination of the employment of the named person ... *(Clause 3·3·3)*

... if ... the employment of the named person is however determined, the Contractor shall notify the Architect ... The Architect shall issue instructions *(Clause 3·3·3)*

MW 80   There are no provisions for named persons as sub-contractors. Architects are advised not to rely on inserting provisional sums for this purpose, as there might be valid resistance from contractors objecting to a subsequent instruction to name.

Fig 3.4.2   Naming: Procedure (2) (Clause 3·3·2)

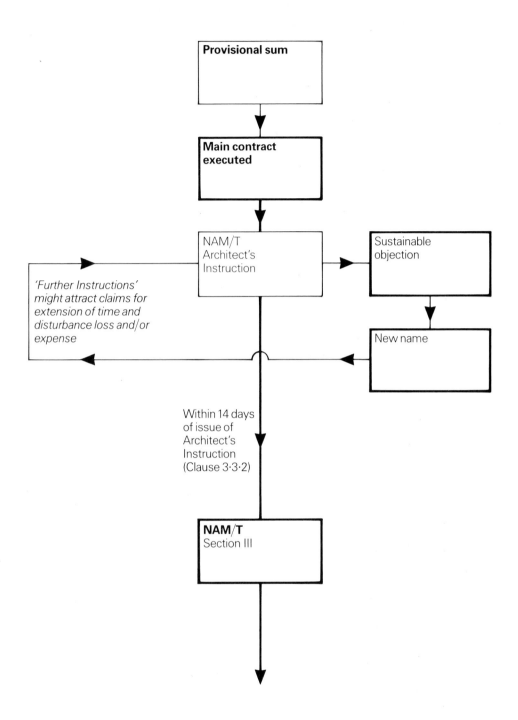

Fig 3.4.3   **Specimen letter of invitation to tender**   For use with IFC 84
                  for named sub-contract works

Base on relevant NJCC Code of Procedure. Assume that preliminary
enquiries have been made. Refer to CASEC *Guide to IFC 84* including
Form NAM/T.

We note that you wish to tender for the above works. We enclose:

- (three) copies of the Form of Tender and Agreement NAM/T;
- one copy each of the 'numbered documents';
- an addressed envelope for the return of the Tender NAM/T.

Please note that:

1   Drawings and details relating to the main contract may be
     inspected at (address) by arrangement with this office.

2   The site may be inspected by arrangement with
     (architect/employer/contractor) at (address).

3   Tendering procedures will be in accordance with the relevant
     NJCC Code of Procedure for selective tendering.

4   The Form of Tender NAM/T should be completed fully and
     properly in Section II.

5   You will be required to enter into Agreement ESA/1 direct
     with the employer.

6   You should send three completed Forms of Tender NAM/T in the
     enclosed envelope to reach this office not later than 12
     noon on (date). The priced documents will be required later,
     if you are nominated to execute the sub-contract works.

Please confirm that you have received this letter and enclosures
and that you are able to tender in accordance with these
instructions.

Fig 3.4.4   **Specimen AI for naming a sub-contractor**   For use with IFC 84
               (Procedure 2, Clause 3·3·2)

Issued by: **Architect's**
address: **instruction**

Employer: Serial no:
address:
                                                Job reference:

Contractor: Issue date:
address:
                                               Contract dated:

Works:
Situated at:

Under the terms of the above Contract, I/We issue the following instructions:

	Office use: Approx costs	
	£ omit	£ add

EXPENDITURE OF PROVISIONAL SUM FOR
NAMED PERSON AS SUB-CONTRACTOR

    OMIT provisional sum of £ ....., under (item) on (page)
    of the Bills of Quantities.

    ADD the sum of £ ....., as shown in the attached tender
    of (date) from (name) on NAM/T.

This Instruction is issued in accordance with clause 3.3.2
of the contract, and is to be valued in accordance with
clause 3.8 of the contract.

You should now enter into a sub-contract on Section III of
NAM/T and in accordance with the enclosed 'Numbered
Documents' and 'Priced Documents'.

To be signed by or for
the issuer named
above.   Signed _____

Amount of Contract Sum   £
± Approximate value of previous instructions   £ _____
                                              £
± Approximate value of this instruction   £ _____
Approximate adjusted total   £

Distribution   ☐ Employer   ☐ Contractor   ☐ Quantity Surveyor   ☐ Services Engineer

             ☐   ☐ Nominated   ☐ Structural Engineer   ☐ File
                              Sub-Contractors

In JCT contracts the term 'nominated sub-contractors' is restricted to JCT 80 and the Fixed Fee Form of Prime Cost Contract. Nominated sub-contractors are not classed as domestic sub-contractors, and the main contractor is not wholly responsible for their performance. They are specialist firms nominated to carry out and complete works against the provisions of prime cost sums included in the contract bills. Nomination may also be made by issuing an Architect's Instruction concerning the expenditure of provisional sums.

Nomination is generally held to be reasonable where:
·   special expertise is required;
·   special quality is required, or
·   time is an important consideration, and long lead times for delivery or fabrication must be accommodated.

The nomination process is ingenious in that it creates a chain of responsibility. The arrangement is useful in practice but awkward in law. The conditions of the JCT standard form are intended to reconcile law with practice. The architect chooses the sub-contractor, but the contractor has a right of reasonable objection. The architect must instruct the contractor to enter into the sub-contract and, if the first sub-contract fails, issue further instructions. The contractor is ultimately responsible for workmanship and materials, but cannot be instructed to carry out the sub-contract works himself. Normally this can only be done by a nominated sub-contractor.

The procedural rules in the contract are inevitably elaborate. They must be followed meticulously.

Volume 1
Action checklists
C2.1 (70), D2.1 (70),
E2.1 (70), F2.1 (70),
G2.1 (70), H2.1 (70)

JCT 80

Clause 35
There are two routes to nomination: the basic method and the alternative method.

The basic method
aims to achieve complete agreement between main contractor and sub-contractor before the architect can formally nominate. (The use of NSC/1, NSC/2, NSC/3 and NSC/4 is obligatory.)

The alternative method
allows the architect to nominate, leaving the main contractor and sub-contractor to reach agreement before executing NSC/4a. It is normal to use NSC/2a, but this can be avoided (Clause 35·11·1). Forms NSC/1a (form of tender) and NSC/3a (form of nomination) are available and although not obligatory, their use is recommended.

The basic method is safest where a high level of integration is needed, and is the norm in the absence of anything to the contrary. This method is defined in Clauses 35·6 to 35·10, preceded by reference to the use of NSC/1 and NSC/2 (Clause 35·5·1). If the alternative method, referred to in Clause 35·5·1·2 and 35·11 to 35·12, is to be used, this must normally be stated when tenders are being invited. It is possible to transfer from one method to the other (Clause 35·5·2) provided that there is time to do this and that the proper procedures are followed.

Fig 3.5.1   Nomination of sub-contractors (Basic Method)

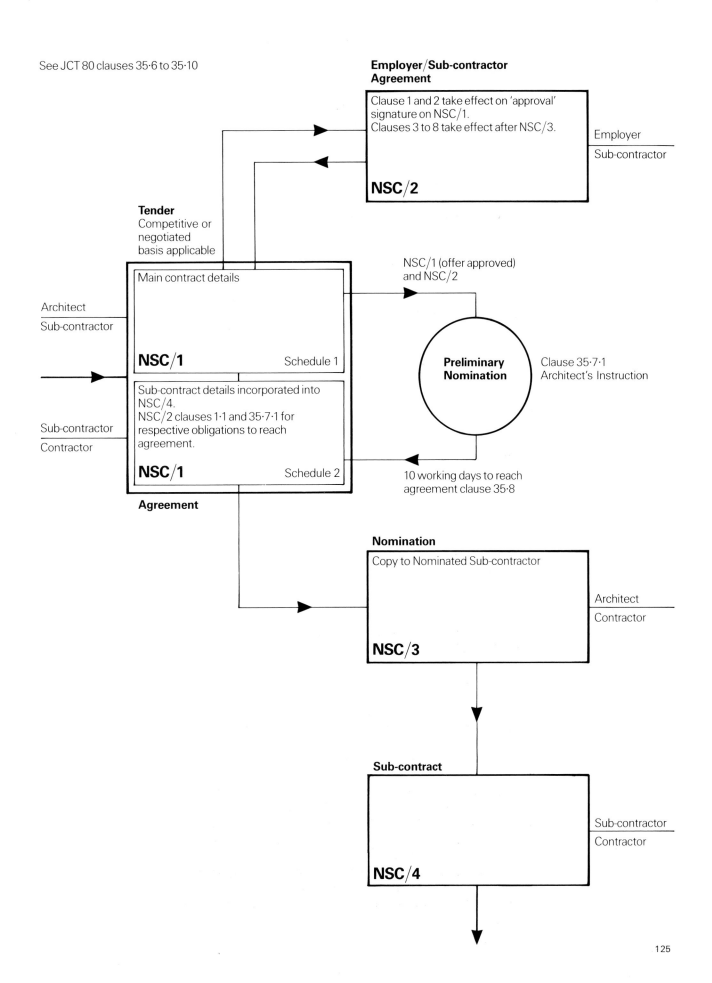

See JCT 80 clauses 35·6 to 35·10

Employer/Sub-contractor Agreement

Clause 1 and 2 take effect on 'approval' signature on NSC/1.
Clauses 3 to 8 take effect after NSC/3.

NSC/2

Employer
Sub-contractor

Tender
Competitive or negotiated basis applicable

Main contract details

NSC/1   Schedule 1

Architect
Sub-contractor

Sub-contractor
Contractor

Sub-contract details incorporated into NSC/4.
NSC/2 clauses 1·1 and 35·7·1 for respective obligations to reach agreement.

NSC/1   Schedule 2

Agreement

NSC/1 (offer approved) and NSC/2

Preliminary Nomination

Clause 35·7·1
Architect's Instruction

10 working days to reach agreement clause 35·8

Nomination

Copy to Nominated Sub-contractor

NSC/3

Architect
Contractor

Sub-contract

NSC/4

Sub-contractor
Contractor

The main contractor may tender for nominated sub-contract work provided that he has the necessary expertise 'ordinarily' within his own organisation (Clause 35·2·1). Such works should be agreed prior to executing the contract, and expressly referred to in the Appendix.

Where provisional sums are included, the architect must issue instructions (Clause 13·3). Instructions are required for a first nomination, for further nomination should a sub-contract not eventuate (Clause 35·23) and for re-nominating a 'substituted sub-contractor' where necessary (Clause 35·18). The main contractor cannot on his own initiative enter into a sub-contract reserved for a nominated sub-contractor.

The risk is that the main contractor will exercise his right of reasonable objection (Clause 35·4·1) or that, despite the obligations under Clause 35·7·2 and Clause 1·1 of NSC/2, the parties may fail to reach agreement (Clause 35·8). The sub-contractor can also rely on the 'Stipulations' of NSC/1 to withdraw an offer, even after being 'approved' by the employer. In all such cases, a new nomination instruction may be required.

Clause 35 contains complex procedures for paying nominated sub-contractors (Clause 35·13), including
·   direct and final payment (Clause 35·13 and 35·17)
·   practical completion (Clause 35·16)
·   failure to complete (Clause 35·15)
·   extensions of time (Clause 35·14)
·   determination (Clause 35·25).

These detailed procedures must be followed meticulously.

Where ... the Architect has, whether by use of a prime cost sum or by naming a Sub-Contractor, reserved to himself the final selection and approval ... the Sub-Contractor ... shall be nominated ... *(Clause 35·1)*

Where ... a proposed Sub-Contractor has tendered on Tender NSC/1 and entered into Agreement NSC/2 the Architect ... shall send to the Contractor ... NSC/1 duly completed, a copy of Agreement NSC/2 and a preliminary notice of nomination ... *(Clause 35·7·1)*

... the Contractor shall forthwith proceed to settle ... any of the Particular Conditions in Schedule 2 of the Tender NSC/1 which remain to be agreed. *(Clause 35·7·2)*

If the Contractor is unable within 10 working days ... to reach agreement ...the Contractor shall continue to comply with clause 35·7 but inform the Architect ... and the Architect shall issue such instructions as may be necessary. *(Clause 35·8)*

Immediately upon settlement ... the Contractor shall send the duly completed Tender NSC/1 ... to the Architect. *(Clause 35·10·1)*

Upon receipt ... the Architect shall forthwith issue an instruction on Nomination NSC/3. *(Clause 35·10·2)*

Where clause 35·5·1·2 has been operated: the Employer shall enter into Agreement NSC2/a ... the Architect shall issue an instruction ... nominating the proposed Sub-Contractor ... *(Clause 35·11)*

The Contractor shall ... conclude a sub-contract ... on Sub-Contract NSC/4a ... within 14 days ... *(Clause 35·12)*

The Contractor shall not grant to any Nominated Sub-Contractor any extension ... which requires the written consent of the Architect ... *(Clause 35·14)*

If any Nominated Sub-Contractor fails to complete ... within the period ... and the Contractor so notifies the Architect ... then provided that the Architect is satisfied that Clause 35·14 has been properly applied ... the Architect shall so certify... *(Clause 35·15·1)*

The certificate of the Architect ... shall be issued not later than 2 months from the date of notification ... *(Clause 35·15·2)*

When in the opinion of the Architect ... practical completion ... by a Nominated Sub-Contractor is achieved he shall forthwith issue a certificate ... *(Clause 35·16)*

The Architect shall ... issue an instruction ... (where proposed nomination does not proceed further) *(Clause 35·23)*

If ... the Contractor informs the Architect ... and the Architect is reasonably of the opinion that the (Nominated) Sub-Contractor has made default ... the Architect shall issue an instruction to the Contractor to give to the Sub-Contractor the notice specifying the default ... and may in that instruction state that the Contractor must obtain a further instruction ... before determining ... *(Clause 35·24)*

If the Contractor informs ... the Architect that the employment of the (Nominated) Sub-Contractor has been so determined the Architect shall make such further nomination ... as may be necessary ... *(Clause 35·24)*

IFC 84   There is no provision for nominated sub-contractors in the conditions.

MW 80   There is no provision for nominated sub-contractors in the conditions.

Fig 3.5.2   Nomination of sub-contractors (Alternative Method)

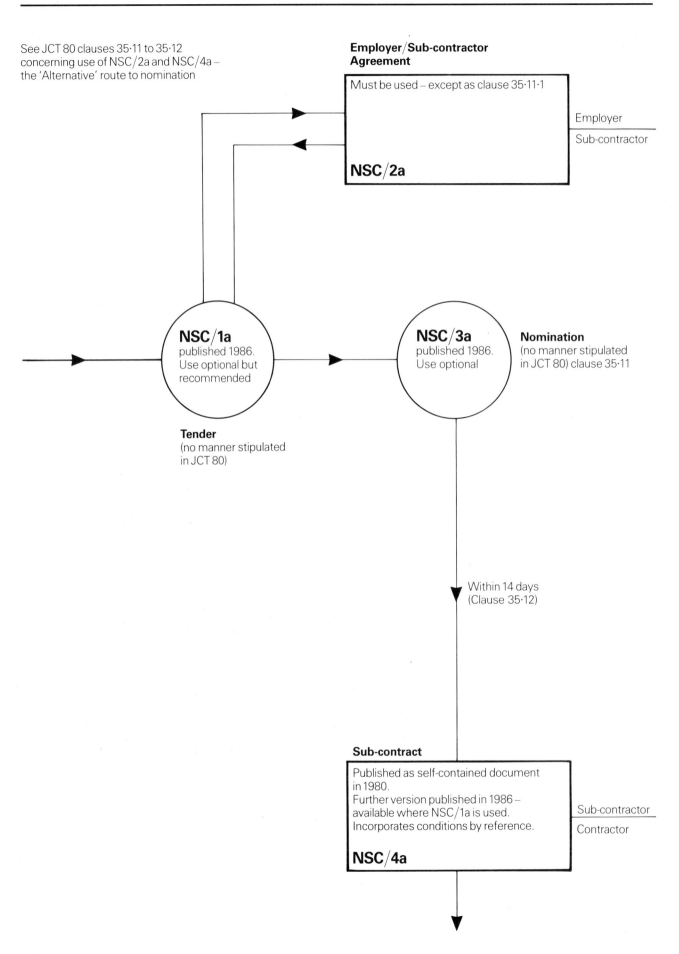

See JCT 80 clauses 35·11 to 35·12
concerning use of NSC/2a and NSC/4a –
the 'Alternative' route to nomination

**Employer/Sub-contractor
Agreement**

Must be used – except as clause 35·11·1

NSC/2a

Employer

Sub-contractor

NSC/1a
published 1986.
Use optional but
recommended

Tender
(no manner stipulated
in JCT 80)

NSC/3a
published 1986.
Use optional

Nomination
(no manner stipulated
in JCT 80) clause 35·11

Within 14 days
(Clause 35·12)

Sub-contract

Published as self-contained document
in 1980.
Further version published in 1986 –
available where NSC/1a is used.
Incorporates conditions by reference.

NSC/4a

Sub-contractor

Contractor

Fig 3.5.3   **Specimen letter of invitation to tender**   For use with JCT 80
                       for nominated sub-contract works

For use with JCT 80 using Form of Tender NSC/1, and NSC/2, the
Employer/Nominated Sub-contractor Agreement, under the Basic
Method of nomination.

Where the Alternative Method is to be used, substitute NSC/1a for
NSC/1, and NSC/2a for NSC/2.

We invite you to prepare and submit a tender for the above works
by 12 noon on (date) in accordance with the information and
conditions stated in this letter and attachments. We enclose:

.   three copies of the Form of Tender NSC/1;
.   two copies of the Form of Employer/Nominated Sub-contractor
     Agreement, NSC/2;
.   and one copy each of Drawings (nos.), Specification (ref.),
     and Bills of Quantities (ref.).

Please note the following:
(delete/amend these items as appropriate)

1   You may inspect drawings and details relating to the main
     contract at these offices by appointment.

2   Visits to the site may be arranged with this office.

3   Tendering procedures will be in accordance with the NJCC
     Code of Procedure for selective tendering.

4   The examination and adjustment of the priced bills will be
     in accordance with Alternative (1 or 2) of section 6 of the
     NJCC Code.

5   All specialists' drawings should be submitted to us in
     duplicate for inspection before fabrication begins.

6   Any specialist drawings prepared before the tender is
     accepted should be submitted to us direct; any prepared
     after the tender is accepted should be submitted to the
     contractor.

7   We will assist in checking specialists' drawings, but any
     failure on our part to detect inconsistencies or errors will
     not relieve sub-contractors of responsibility.

You should complete the relevant parts of Form NSC/1 and sign the
copies; sign the two copies of NSC/2, and return the forms
(retaining a copy of NSC/1 for your records) in the addressed
envelope provided by the date stated above.

Copy to: quantity surveyor, consultants

Tender NSC/1

 JCT Standard Form of Nominated Sub-Contract Tender and Agreement (Amended January 1987)

See "Notes on the Completion of Tender NSC/1" on page 2.

Main Contract Works:[a]   Job reference:

Location:

Sub-Contract Works:

To: The Employer and Main Contractor [a]

We _____

of _____

_____ Tel. No: _____

offer, *upon and subject to the stipulations overleaf*, to carry out and complete, as a Nominated Sub-Contractor and as part of the Main Contract Works referred to above, the Sub-Contract Works identified above in accordance with *the drawings/specifications/bills of quantities/schedule of rates for the Sub-Contract Works which are annexed hereto, numbered

and signed by ourselves and by the Architect/Supervising Officer; and the Particular Conditions set out in Schedule 2 when agreed with the Main Contractor; and JCT Sub-Contract NSC/4 which incorporates the particulars of the Main Contract set out in Schedule 1.

*for the VAT-exclusive Sub-Contract Sum of £ _____

_____ (words)

or *for the VAT-exclusive Tender Sum of [b] £ _____

_____ (words)

The daywork percentages (Sub-Contract NSC/4 clause 16·3·4 or clause 17·4·3) are:

Definition*[c]	Labour %	Materials %	Plant %
RICS/NFBTE			
RICS/ECA			
RICS/ECA (Scotland)			
RICS/HVCA			

The Sub-Contract Sum/Tender Sum and percentages take into account the 2½% cash discount allowable to the Main Contractor under Sub-Contract NSC/4.

Signed by or on behalf of the Sub-Contractor   Date

Approved by the Architect/Supervising Officer
on behalf of the Employer   Date

ACCEPTED by or on behalf of the Main Contractor
subject to a nomination instruction on Nomination NSC/3
under clause 35·10 of the Main Contract Conditions   Date

© 1987 RIBA Publications Ltd   *Delete as applicable   **Page 1**

Fig 3.5.5	**Specimen letter to employer** concerning the completion of Agreement NSC/2 (Basic Method)	For use with JCT 80

For use with JCT 80 under the Basic Method of nomination. Where
the Alternative Method is to be used, substitute NSC/2a for NSC/2,
and clause references 1·1 and 1·2 for 2·1 and 2·2; clauses 3 and 4 for 4
and 5; and clause 6 for clause 7.

We enclose the JCT Standard Form of Employer/Nominated Sub-
Contractor Agreement, NSC/2, which has been completed by the
proposed sub-contractor in connection with the (above work).

We draw your attention to the following clauses:

2.1   the sub-contractor warrants to use reasonable care and
skill, and this becomes operative as soon as you sign
this form;

2.2   you can authorise us to instruct the sub-contractor to
undertake work in advance, but this would entail
certain obligations;

4, 5, 7   these clauses concern your agreement to
direct payment under certain circumstances (but your
interests are safeguarded).

Please sign and date Agreement NSC/2 and have your signature
witnessed; then return the document to us. If there are any
aspects that you wish us to clarify further, we will be glad to
do so.

Copy to: quantity surveyor, consultants

Issued by:
address:

Employer:
address:

Contractor:
address:

Works:
Situated at:

**Architect's
instruction**

Serial no:

Job reference:

Issue date:

Contract dated:

Under the terms of the above Contract, I/We issue the following instructions:

	Office use: Approx costs	
PRELIMINARY NOTICE OF NOMINATION	£ omit	£ add

PRELIMINARY NOTICE OF NOMINATION

    OMIT provisional sum of £ ....., under (item) on (page)
of the Bills of Quantities.

    ADD the sum of £ ......, as shown on the attached
tender of (date) from (name) on NSC/1.

This is a Preliminary Nomination Instruction issued under
clause 35.7 of the contract. Please agree with this proposed
sub-contractor the matters relevant to Schedule 2 of NSC/1,
and return the completed tender so that we can issue the
Nomination Instruction on Form NSC/3.

To be signed by or for
the issuer named
above.

Signed _____

Amount of Contract Sum	£	
± Approximate value of previous instructions	£	_____
	£	
± Approximate value of this instruction	£	_____
Approximate adjusted total	£	

Distribution ☐ Employer   ☐ Contractor   ☐ Quantity Surveyor   ☐ Services Engineer

☐   ☐ Nominated   ☐ Structural Engineer   ☐ File
                            Sub-Contractors

© 1985 RIBA Publications Ltd

Fig 3.5.7   Specimen letter to nominated sub-contractor   For use with JCT 80
concerning preliminary nomination (Basic Method)

We have today issued a preliminary nomination to the main
contractor, (name), on the basis of your offer stated in Forms
NSC/1 and NSC/2 and in accordance with clause 35 of the contract.

Please resolve with the contractor any outstanding matters
relating to Schedule 2 of NSC/1 within 10 days. If you have any
difficulty in completing NSC/1, you should inform the contractor
immediately.

Do not order any materials or carry out any work until we make
the formal nomination or issue further instructions.

Copy to: quantity surveyor

3.5 **Nominated Sub-Contractors**

Fig 3.5.8   Specimen AI withdrawing preliminary nomination where   For use with JCT 80
approved NSC does not wish to proceed

Issued by:
address:

Employer:
address:

Contractor:
address:

Works:
Situated at:

Architect's instruction

Serial no:

Job reference:

Issue date:

Contract dated:

Under the terms of the above Contract, I/We issue the following instructions:

	Office use: Approx costs	
	£ omit	£ add

```
WITHDRAWAL OF PRELIMINARY NOMINATION OF (name)
AS NOMINATED SUB-CONTRACTOR FOR (type of work)

We withdraw our Preliminary Nomination issued under
Architect's Instruction (no.) of (date).

This Instruction is issued in accordance with clause 35.9 of
the contract.
```

To be signed by or for
the issuer named
above.

Signed _____

Amount of Contract Sum	£	
± Approximate value of previous instructions	£	_____
	£	
± Approximate value of this instruction	£	_____
Approximate adjusted total	£	

Distribution

☐ Employer   ☐ Contractor   ☐ Quantity Surveyor   ☐ Services Engineer

☐   ☐ Nominated Sub-Contractors   ☐ Structural Engineer   ☐ File

Fig 3.5.9   **Specimen AI withdrawing nomination after reasonable objection by contractor (Alternative Method)**   For use with JCT 80

Issued by:
address:

Employer:
address:

Contractor:
address:

Works:
Situated at:

Architect's instruction

Serial no:

Job reference:

Issue date:

Contract dated:

Under the terms of the above Contract, I/We issue the following instructions:

	Office use: Approx costs	
	£ omit	£ add
WITHDRAWAL OF NOMINATION OF (name) AS NOMINATED SUB-CONTRACTOR FOR (type of work) We withdraw our Nomination issued under Architect's Instruction (no.)/NSC/3a of (date). This Instruction is issued in accordance with clause 35.23 of the contract.		

To be signed by or for the issuer named above.

Signed _____

Amount of Contract Sum	£
± Approximate value of previous instructions	£ _____
	£
± Approximate value of this instruction	£ _____
Approximate adjusted total	£

Distribution ☐ Employer   ☐ Contractor   ☐ Quantity Surveyor   ☐ Services Engineer

☐   ☐ Nominated Sub-Contractors   ☐ Structural Engineer   ☐ File

© 1985 RIBA Publications Ltd

Fig 3.5.10   Specimen letter to contractor   For use with JCT 80
rejecting objection to nomination of sub-contractor
(Alternative Method)

> We have carefully considered the matters you raised in your
> letter of (date), but we do not agree that they constitute
> reasonable grounds for objecting to this nomination under clause
> 35.4 of the contract.
>
> We trust that you will reconsider your objections and proceed
> with the sub-contract as instructed.
>
>
> Copy to: quantity surveyor, consultant

Fig 3.5.11   Specimen letter to employer   For use with JCT 80
concerning renomination following determination of
nominated sub-contractor

> We regret to inform you that the employment of the nominated sub-
> contractor for the (type of work) has been determined.
>
> The contractor notified default in accordance with clause 35.24.1
> of the contract, and after investigation we instructed the
> contractor to serve formal notice specifying the default on the
> nominated sub-contractor in accordance with clause 35.24.5.1. The
> contractor has now determined the employment of the nominated
> sub-contractor in accordance with clause 29 of the sub-contract
> following the continuation of the default.
>
> It is now necessary to nominate another sub-contractor to
> complete the works, as required by clause 35.24.5.3 of the
> contract. We are making enquiries and will keep you informed.
>
>
> Copy to: quantity surveyor, consultant

Fig 3.5.12   **Specimen letter to contractor**   For use with JCT 80
requesting reasonable proof of discharge of payment to
nominated sub-contractors

May we draw your attention to the procedures clearly stated in
the contract concerning your obligation to provide reasonable
proof of discharge.

Following the issue of Interim Certificate (no.) on (date) and in
accordance with clause 35.13 of the contract, please confirm that
you have discharged the payment due to the nominated sub-
contractor, (name).

To avoid delays in processing Interim Certificates in future,
please send us in good time the nominated sub-contractors'
acknowledgments of payment, or other evidence of discharge.

Copy to: quantity surveyor, consultant (if appropriate)

The term 'nominated suppliers' is only used in JCT 80. Suppliers of goods or materials are nominated against prime cost sums included in the contract bills, or by issuing an Architect's Instruction concerning the expenditure of provisional sums.

Nomination ensures that the contractor uses goods of a particular design and quality from a particular source, and that he purchases them under a contract of sale which contains certain terms.

It is common practice to refer to specific supply items even when contracts do not expressly allow for this. Make sure that the items are available on reasonable delivery before naming them in the contract documents. Where time is of the essence, only approve quotations where delivery dates are guaranteed.

Volume 1
Action checklists
C2.1 (70), D2.1 (70),
E2.1 (70), F2.1 (70),
G2.1 (70), H2.1 (70)

JCT 80

Clause 36

Clause 36 contains a definition which clarifies that where there is a provisional sum or prime cost sum, a named supplier is nominated. Where nomination is effected under an Architect's Instruction concerning the expenditure of a provisional sum or requiring a variation, then materials or goods must be covered by a prime cost sum. Where goods and materials can only be obtained from one source, they will not be classed as 'nominated' unless a provisional sum or prime cost sum is included in the contract.

The architect must issue instructions concerning nomination. The sales contract for the goods or materials must include the conditions expressly set out in Clause 36, although these may be relaxed with the agreement in writing of the architect and the contractor, whose liability is then limited accordingly. Provided the conditions of Clause 36 are complied with, the contractor has no right of objection.

The use of JCT Form of Tender TNS/1 is recommended together with Warranty TNS/2.

> The Architect shall issue instructions ... nominating a supplier ... *(Clause 36·2)*
>
> Nothing ... shall be construed as enabling the Architect to nominate ... otherwise than in accordance with ... clause 36·4. *(Clause 36·5·3)*.

IFC 84

There is no provision for nominating suppliers.

MW 80

There is no provision for nominating suppliers.

Fig 3.6.1   **Specimen letter of invitation to tender by nominated suppliers**   For use with JCT 80

The use of forms TNS/1, Tender for Nominated Suppliers, and TNS/2, Warranty for Nominated Suppliers, is not required under JCT 80. However, they are a convenient vehicle for presenting the relevant information and conditions, and the use of TNS/2 is advisable whenever a design warranty and an assurance of delivery by a specified date is important.

We invite your tender for supplying the (above items) in accordance with the requirements shown on the (drawings, extracts from bills/specification/schedules etc.) listed below.

Your tender should be set out on the enclosed form of tender, TNS/1, and be accompanied by the form of warranty, TNS/2, and your relevant technical drawings, specifications and schedules. By signing the forms you will acknowledge that no terms or conditions other than those in Clause 36 of JCT 80 are to apply.

Please note that all specialists' drawings are to be presented in duplicate to us in reasonable time for inspection and comment before any work is fabricated. We will check these drawings only so far as their coordination and integration into the overall design is concerned. Any failure on our part to detect inconsistencies or errors will not relieve you of full responsibility for the competence, proper execution and performance of your work.

Please describe clearly all attendance and associated works that have be carried out by the contractor, such as unloading, protection, scaffolding, builder's supplies and works necessary for placing/fixing your products. You should include full installation and maintenance instructions.

Your tender should reach this office not later than 12 noon on (date) and be clearly marked 'TENDER - For the attention of (name)'.

If you are unable to quote, please return these documents immediately. This will not prejudice your opportunities for future work.

Copy to: quantity surveyor, consultants

Tender TNS/1

JCT Standard Form of Tender by Nominated Supplier

For use in connection with the Standard Form of Building Contract (SFBC) issued by the Joint Contracts Tribunal, 1980 edition, current revision

Job Title:
(name and brief location of Works)

[a] To be completed by or on behalf of the Architect/Supervising Officer.

Employer:[a]

Main Contractor:[a]
(if known)

Tender for:[a]
(abbreviated description)

Name of Tenderer:

To be returned to:[a]

[b] To be completed by the supplier; see also Schedule 1, item 7.

Lump sum price:[b] £ _____

_____ (words)

and/or Schedule of rates (attached)

1   We confirm that we will be under a contract with the Main Contractor:

·1   to supply the materials or goods described or referred to in **Schedule 1** for the price and/or at the rate set out above; and

·2   in accordance with the other terms set out in that Schedule, as a Nominated Supplier in accordance with the terms of SFBC clause 36·3 to ·5 (as set out in **Schedule 2**) and our conditions of sale in so far as they do not conflict with the terms of SFBC clause 36·3 to ·5 [c]

[c] By SFBC clause 36·4·9 none of the provisions in the contract of sale can override, modify or affect in any way the provisions incorporated from SFBC clause 36·4 in that contract of sale. Nominated Suppliers should therefore take steps to ensure that their sale conditions do not incorporate any provisions which purport to override, modify or affect in any way the provisions incorporated from SFBC clause 36·4.

provided:

·3   the Architect/Supervising Officer has issued the relevant nomination instruction (a copy of which has been sent to us by the Architect/Supervising Officer); and

·4   agreement on delivery between us and the Main Contractor has been reached as recorded in **Schedule 1** Part 6 (see SFBC clause 36·4·3); and

·5   we have thereafter received an order from the Main Contractor accepting this tender.

2   We agree that this Tender shall be open for acceptance by an order from the Main Contractor within   [d] of the date of this Tender. Provided that where the Main Contractor has not been named above we reserve the right to withdraw this Tender within 14 days of having been notified, by or on behalf of the Employer named above, of the name of the Main Contractor.

[d] May be completed by or on behalf of the Architect/Supervising Officer; if not so completed, to be completed by the supplier.

[e] To be struck out by or on behalf of the Architect/Supervising Officer if no Warranty Agreement is required.

3[e]   Subject to our right to withdraw this Tender as set out in paragraph 2 we hereby declare that we accept the Warranty Agreement in the terms set out in **Schedule 3** hereto on condition that no provision in that Warranty Agreement shall take effect unless and until

a copy to us of the instruction nominating us,
the order of the Main Contractor accepting this Tender, and
a copy of the Warranty Agreement signed by the Employer

have been received by us.

For and on behalf of

Address

Signature   Date

Page 1

Fig 3.6.3   JCT Form of Warranty for Nominated Suppliers, TNS/2

Schedule 3 : Warranty by a Nominated Supplier

To the Employer:
named in our Tender dated

For:
(abbreviated description of goods/materials)

To be supplied to:
(job title)

1   Subject to the conditions stated in the above mentioned Tender (that no provision in this Warranty
     Agreement shall take effect unless and until the instruction nominating us, the order of the Main
     Contractor accepting the Tender and a copy of this Warranty Agreement signed by the Employer have
     been received by us) WE WARRANT in consideration of our being nominated in respect of the supply
     of the goods and/or materials to be supplied by us as a Nominated Supplier under the Standard Form
     of Building Contract referred to in the Tender and in accordance with the description, quantity and quality
     of the materials or goods and with the other terms and details set out in the Tender ('the supply') that:

1·1   We have exercised and will exercise all reasonable skill and care in:

1·1   ·1   the design of the supply insofar as the supply has been or will be designed by us; and

       ·2   the selection of materials and goods for the supply insofar as such supply has been or will be selected
            by us; and

       ·3   the satisfaction of any performance specification or requirement insofar as such performance
            specification or requirement is included or referred to in the Tender as part of the description
            of the supply.

1·2   We will:

1·2   ·1   save insofar as we are delayed by:

            ·1·1 force majeure; or

            ·1·2 civil commotion, local combination of workmen, strike or lock-out; or

            ·1·3 any instruction of the Architect/Supervising Officer under SFBC clause 13·2 (Variations) or
                  clause 13·3 (provisional sums); or

            ·1·4 failure of the Architect/Supervising Officer to supply to us within due time any necessary
                  information for which we have specifically applied in writing on a date which was neither
                  unreasonably distant from nor unreasonably close to the date on which it was necessary for
                  us to receive the same

            so supply the Architect/Supervising Officer with such information as the Architect/Supervising
            Officer may reasonably require; and

       ·2   so supply the Contractor with such information as the Contractor may reasonably require in
            accordance with the arrangements in our contract of sale with the Contractor; and

       ·3   so commence and complete delivery of the supply in accordance with the arrangements in our
            contract of sale with the Contractor

       that the Contractor shall not become entitled to an extension of time under SFBC clauses 25·4·6 or 25·4·7
       of the Main Contract Conditions nor become entitled to be paid for direct loss and/or expense ascertained
       under SFBC clause 26·1 for the matters referred to in clause 26·2·1 of the Main Contract Conditions; and
       we will indemnify you to the extent but not further or otherwise that the Architect/Supervising Officer is
       obliged to give an extension of time so that the Employer is unable to recover damages under the Main
       Contractor for delays in completion, and/or pay an amount in respect of direct loss and/or expense as
       aforesaid because of any failure by us under clause 1·2·1 or 1·2·2 hereof.

Pages 1-4 comprising TNS/1 with Schedules 1 and 2 are issued in
a separate pad.

                                                                                Page 5

Issued by:
address:

Employer:
address:

Contractor:
address:

Works:
Situated at:

Architect's instruction

Serial no:

Job reference:

Issue date:

Contract dated:

Under the terms of the above Contract, I/We issue the following instructions:

	Office use: Approx costs
NOMINATED SUPPLIER FOR IRONMONGERY	£ omit / £ add

OMIT provisional sum of £ ..... under (item) on (page) of the Bills of Quantities.

ADD the sum of £ ....., as shown on the attached tender of (date) from (name) on Forms TNS/1 and TNS/2.

This Instruction is issued under clause 36.2 of the contract.

To be signed by or for the issuer named above.

Signed _____

Amount of Contract Sum £
± Approximate value of previous instructions £ _____
£
± Approximate value of this instruction £ _____
Approximate adjusted total £

Distribution ☐ Employer ☐ Contractor ☐ Quantity Surveyor ☐ Services Engineer
☐ ☐ Nominated Sub-Contractors ☐ Structural Engineer ☐ File

© 1985 RIBA Publications Ltd

The contract conditions must imply a right of reasonable access so that the architect can ensure that the contract conditions are being complied with and issue any certificates required.

Contracts do not normally refer to any rights of the employer to visit the site. It may be helpful for the architect to suggest to the employer that should he wish to visit the site, he should be accompanied by the architect. This would be in the interests of safety and would also provide an opportunity for him to be properly informed about the work.

Unless otherwise agreed, legitimate access is usually restricted to normal working hours. The contract conditions may also oblige the contractor to secure a similar right of access in connection with sub-contractors' work, if this is possible.

JCT 80

Clause 11
The architect and his representatives must be allowed access to the works and workshops of the contractor at all reasonable times. The contractor should secure similar access for sub-contractors if possible. Note that access may be restricted to protect any proprietary rights. There is no mention of access to suppliers.

> The Architect ... shall at all reasonable times have access to the works and to the workshops...
>
> Access ... may be subject to such reasonable restrictions ... as are necessary to protect any proprietary right ...
> *(Clause 11)*

IFC 84

There is no provision for access. Sub-contract NAM/SC Clause 23 does expressly refer to the right of access by the architect and duly authorised persons in respect of sub-contract works.

MW 80

There is no provision for access in the conditions.

3.8   Person-in-Charge

The contractor is wholly responsible for site supervision, which must be constant and proper. He is required to appoint a competent person-in-charge. Should he fail to do so, or fail to notify the person's name, an appropriate letter should be sent by the architect.

Volume 1
J6 Initial Project Meeting

The person-in-charge (general foreman or site agent) should keep a detailed site diary, recording weather and site conditions, deliveries of materials, plant and equipment, details of the work force, information received or outstanding, visitors to the site and the progress of the works in relation to the programme. He should be present at the initial project meeting and be properly briefed on procedures concerning progress, quality control, AIs, valuations, and so on.

JCT 80

Clause 1·4
The architect is not responsible for the supervision of the works, nor for the quality of work achieved on site. The contractor is wholly responsible, and this obligation is in no way reduced because the architect makes site visits, or includes work and materials for payment under interim certificates, or because there is a clerk of works.

Clause 10
The contractor is required to maintain a competent person-in-charge on the site authorised to receive instructions from the architect and directions from the clerk of works. The contractor should name the appointee before site operations start, and should notify the architect of any change proposed during the contract.

> The Contractor shall constantly keep upon the works a competent person-in-charge ... *(Clause 10)*

IFC 84

Clause 3·4
The contractor is required to keep a competent person-in-charge on the site at all reasonable times.

> The Contractor shall at all reasonable times keep upon the works a competent person-in-charge ... *(Clause 3·4)*

MW 80

Clause 3·3
The contractor is required to keep a competent person-in-charge on the site at all reasonable times.

> The Contractor shall at all reasonable times keep upon the works a competent person-in-charge ... *(Clause 3·3)*

The architect is sometimes required to exclude a person or persons from the works. This could be because of incompetence or misconduct, or because the person is exerting an undesirable influence upon the standard or progress of the works. The word 'person' may be taken to include both natural persons and artificial persons, such as corporation or company.

Sometimes it may also be necessary (where, for instance, there is a high security risk or particular circumstances associated with health or welfare buildings) to ensure that site operatives keep apart from other people on or near the site.

This provision should be exercised with discretion. It would be diplomatic to raise any such matter with the contractor before taking any action. Remember that the word 'exclude' should be used (not 'dismissed'), or there may be problems with current employment legislation.

JCT 80

Clause 8·5
The architect may issue instructions concerning the exclusion from the works of any person employed there. Such notice must not be given unreasonably or vexatiously.

The architect would be wise not to give reasons in the written instructions. The definition in the contract (Clause 1·3) makes it clear that the clause covers individuals, firms and corporate bodies.

> The Architect may ... issue instructions requiring ... exclusion from the works ... *(Clause 8·5)*

IFC 84

There is no provision for exclusion in the conditions.

MW 80

Clause 3·4 carries an identical provision to Clause 8·5 of JCT 80.

> The Architect may ... issue instructions requiring ... exclusion from the works ... *(Clause 3·4)*

In most contracts only the architect has the power to issue instructions. All instructions from consultants must therefore be channelled through the architect and issued by him.

The architect's powers to issue instructions are subject to the terms of the contract and may therefore be limited. The contractor is only obliged to comply with valid instructions.

Under the contract the architect may have discretionary powers to issue some instructions, and be obliged to issue others. In the absence of anything specific in the contract, such instructions should be issued within a reasonable time. Failure to issue necessary instructions could be a breach of contract by the employer through his agent, the architect.

Instructions should be in writing, and the architect should agree with the contractor at the outset what constitutes a 'proper' instruction, otherwise it may be claimed that such things as minutes, letters and telephone calls have the status of instructions. The wording of instructions should be meticulously checked and be clear and unambiguous.

Instructions sent by fax, although these are clearly instructions in writing, should nevertheless be confirmed in the normal way using Architect's Instructions. Where there is a fax facility on site, it might be wise to agree with the contractor at the outset how to identify which faxed messages are to be taken as Architect's Instructions. It might also be wise not to respond too hastily to requests for information received via fax from the contractor, in case insufficient time is given to considering fully the implications of such requests.

Consider carefully any possible consequences in terms of disturbance, costs or delay before issuing instructions.

Volume 1
Action checklist J2.1 (70)
J6 Initial Project Meeting

JCT 80

Clause 4·1

The architect is obliged to issue instructions in respect of certain matters ('shall'), and is *empowered* to issue instructions in respect of others ('may').

The contractor may require the architect to specify the provisions of the contract under which an instruction is issued. These provisions include:

Clause 2·3	Discrepancies or divergences
Clause 6·1	Statutory requirements
Clause 7	Levels and setting out
Clause 8	Materials, goods and workmanship
	Supply of vouchers
	Opening up of work and testing
	Removal of goods or materials
	Exclusion from the works
Clause 9	Royalties and patent rights
Clause 10	Person-in-charge
Clause 11	Access to work
Clause 12	Clerk of works
Clause 13	Variations
Clause 16	Consent to remove goods from site
Clause 17	Practical completion and defects liability period
Clause 18	Partial possession by employer
Clause 19	Domestic sub-contractors
Clause 21	Insurance against injury to persons or property
Clause 22	Insurance of the works
Clause 23	Postponement
Clause 25	Extensions of time
Clause 32	Hostilities
Clause 33	War damage
Clause 34	Antiquities
Clause 35	Nominated sub-contractors
Clause 36	Nominated suppliers

The contractor is required to carry out valid Architect's Instructions forthwith, subject to the right of challenge in Clause 4·2 and the reservation over variations ordered under Clause 13·1·2.

If the contractor fails to carry out instructions, the architect should send a written notice requiring compliance. This should be done within a reasonable time, and should draw the contractor's attention to the likely consequences of continued non-compliance. If non-compliance continues for a further seven days, the employer may employ someone else to carry out the instructions and recover the cost from the contractor. If an employer does not wish to exercise this right immediately, he should be advised to write to the contractor reserving the right to do so later.

Clause 4·3

It should be agreed at the outset what constitutes an instruction. All instructions from the architect must be in writing.

It is recommended that the RIBA form of Architect's Instruction is always used to issue instructions, to confirm all instructions previously given, or to confirm directions given by a clerk of works. Instructions confirming directions by a clerk of works should refer to the date and serial number of the document concerned.

This clause does not specifically mention oral instructions, but refers to 'instructions otherwise than in writing'. All such instructions must be confirmed in writing, referring to the date of the oral instruction and the name of the person to whom it was given.

The RIBA form may be used for instructions which involve a variation, and also for those which do not. The original should be sent to the contractor and copied to others as necessary. The circulation list should be marked clearly to indicate where copies have been supplied. Instructions should be dated and numbered in sequence. In the case of oral instructions given by the architect, the contractor may confirm them in writing within seven days, although if the architect does not dissent within a further period of seven days the instructions shall have effect. The architect may himself confirm oral instructions within seven days. Where work has been carried out by the contractor without written confirmation, the architect may confirm instructions at any time up to the Final Certificate.

The Contractor shall forthwith comply with all instructions issued to him by the Architect ... *(Clause 4·1·1)*

... the Contractor may request the Architect to specify in writing the provisions ... which empower ... the said instruction. The Architect shall forthwith comply ... *(Clause 4·2)*

All instructions ... shall be issued in writing. *(Clause 4·3·1)*

... an instruction otherwise than in writing ... shall be confirmed in writing ... within 7 days ... *(Clause 4·3·2)*

... if neither the Contractor nor the Architect shall confirm ... but the Contractor shall nevertheless comply with the same, then the Architect may confirm ... prior to the Final Certificate ... *(Clause 4·3·2·2)*

IFC 84

Clause 3·5

All instructions by the architect must be in writing. Otherwise, the provisions are broadly similar to Clause 4 of JCT 80.

> All instructions of the Architect shall be in writing ... The Contractor shall forthwith comply ... *(Clause 3·5·1)*
>
> If ... the Contractor does not comply ... then the Employer may employ and pay other persons ... to give effect to such instruction ... *(Clause 3·5·1)*
>
> ... The Contractor may request the Architect to specify in writing the provision ... which empowers ... the said instruction. The Architect shall forthwith comply ... *(Clause 3·5·2)*

MW 80

Clause 3·5

Instructions by the architect must be in writing. Oral instructions are to be confirmed in writing by the architect within two days.

> The Architect may issue written instructions ... if instructions are given orally they shall, in two days. be confirmed in writing ... *(Clause 3·5)*.

Fig 3.10.1

**Specimen letter to contractor
following failure to comply with an AI**

For use with JCT 80

Send by Recorded Delivery

> In accordance with clause 4.1 of the contract, we give notice that you have not complied with Architect's Instruction (no.) of (date), and that if within seven days of receiving this letter you do not do so, the employer may engage and pay others to carry out the Instruction.
>
> All the costs incurred in engaging others to carry out the Instruction may be deducted from monies due or which may become due to you or may be recoverable as a debt.
>
> Copy to: employer, quantity surveyor, consultant, clerk of works

3.11　Variations

In building contracts, the architect's power to order variations must be expressly stated. The term 'variation' generally refers to a change in the type or quantity of work to be carried out. However, some contract conditions expressly empower the architect to impose restrictions on the contractor's method of carrying out the work.

Volume 1
Action checklist J2.1 (70)
J6 Initial Project Meeting

When issuing instructions ordering a variation, the architect must take care to keep strictly within the terms of the contract.

The nature of the contract itself cannot be varied by means of a variation order.

JCT 80

Clause 13·1
The definition of 'variation' includes altering or modifying the work and altering working procedures. The architect's authority to vary work described and priced in the contract bills is limited. He is not entitled to issue instructions nominating a sub-contractor for work described and priced in the bills.

The architect has no authority to vary the conditions of the contract, nor to release the contractor from his obligations under the contract. The conditions can only be changed with the agreement of the employer and the contractor.

Clause 13·2
The architect may issue instructions requiring a variation, or he may sanction a variation made by the contractor without an instruction. The clause states that a variation cannot vitiate a contract, but an unreasonable extension of the duration of the work might be grounds for dispute.

Clause 13·4
Valuation of a variation is either by agreement between the parties or by using the valuation rules set out in Clause 13·5.

> The Architect may issue instructions requiring a variation ...
> *(Clause 13·2)*

IFC 84

Clause 3·6
The definition of variation is broadly as under Clause 13·1 of JCT 80. Valuation is either by prior agreement between the parties or by using the valuation rules set out in Clause 3·7.

> The Architect may issue instructions requiring a variation ...
> *(Clause 3·6)*

MW 80

Clause 3·6

The architect may order an addition to, omission from or other change in the works, or vary the order or period in which they are to be carried out. No definition of a variation is given. Valuation is to be by prior agreement between the architect and the contractor, or on a fair and reasonable basis using, where relevant, the priced documents.

> The Architect may ... order an addition to or omission from or other change ... *(Clause 3·6)*

Fig 3.11.1

Specimen letter to employer about the implications of additional work

For use with MW80

This is simply an attempt to warn the employer of the possible implications of additional work. Obviously the architect's opinion on a revision to the completion date etc will require further detailed investigation.

```
Further to our discussion about the additional work you propose,
may we draw your attention to the following points.

First, the contractor advises us that it will not be possible to
complete the additional work within the contract period. Second,
the quantity surveyor advises us that extra costs are likely to
arise from:

(a)   the cost of the work;
(b)   the extension of the contract period;
(c)   reimbursement for the disturbance to the contractor's
      programme.

If after further consideration you still wish to proceed with
this work, we will submit applications to the planning and
building control authorities on your behalf. These will be
subject to the usual formalities and fees.




Copy to: quantity surveyor, consultant
```

The definition of a *provisional sum* depends on which edition of the Standard Method of Measurement has been used.

According to SMM6:
'A provisional sum is a sum provided for work or for costs which cannot be entirely foreseen, defined or detailed at the time the tendering documents are issued.' *(Item 8.1(a))*

SMM7 refers to two types of provisional sum:

(1) A provisional sum for defined work – for work which is not completely designed but for which the following information shall be provided:
  – the nature and construction of the work;
  – a statement of how and where work is fixed;
  – a quantity to indicate scope and extent;
  – specific limitations *(Rules 10.3 and 10.4)*.

(2) A provisional sum for undefined work – for work where the information required under Rule 10.3 cannot be given *(Rules 10.5 and 10.6)*.

The definition of a *prime cost sum* under SMM6 is:
'A sum provided for work or services to be executed by a nominated sub-contractor, a statutory authority or a public undertaking, for for materials or goods to be obtained from a nominated supplier.' *(Item A8.1(b))*

SMM7 contains no such definition, but refers to 'pc sum' only in A51 (nominated sub-contractors) and A52 (nominated suppliers).

The term 'contingency sum', which is frequently used, does not appear to have any official definition, but it is often inserted as a holding device to meet or offset the cost of works which cannot be foreseen at tender stage. There is no reference to it in the JCT forms of contract.

Volume 1
Action checklists
F2.1(70), G2.1(70), J2.1(70)

JCT 80

Clause 13·3
The architect is required to issue instructions regarding the expenditure of provisional sums in the main contract or a sub-contract. This is expressly referred to in Clause 6 (fees or charges) and Clauses 35 and 36 (nominations).

The instruction to the contractor may be issued under an Architect's Instruction form or, where nominated sub-contractors are concerned, on the appropriate NSC form or with the appropriate TNS documents for nominated suppliers.

When issuing instructions about the expenditure of provisional sums arising out of sub-contracts, note that there are no provisions in JCT 80 or NSC/4 to deal with nominations for further sub-contracting within a nominated sub-contract.

> The Architect shall issue instructions in regard to: the expenditure of provisional sums ... *(Clause 13·3)*

IFC 84

Clause 3·8
The architect is required to issue instructions regarding the expenditure of provisional sums.

Provisional sums are expressly referred to in Clause 3·3 (named persons as sub-contractors).

> The Architect shall issue instructions as to ... any provisional sums. *(Clause 3·8)*

MW 80

Clause 3·7
The architect is required to issue instructions regarding the expenditure of provisional sums.

> The Architect shall issue instructions as to ... any provisional sums ... *(Clause 3·7)*

The contractor is responsible for setting out the works accurately. Boundaries should be carefully defined and exact locations agreed. The architect is responsible for ensuring that the contractor is given accurate information about levels, dimensions, etc to enable him to set out. The architect must issue instructions if the contractor informs him of errors in the drawings.

If the contractor fails to set out the works accurately, he will be in breach of contract and will have to correct any errors at his own expense. In practice, the employer might be prepared to 'trade off' a less than critical error in return for an appropriate deduction from the contract sum. Where matters such as contravention of planning consent, trespass, infringement of rights of light, etc are involved, architects should make investigations and advise the employer accordingly.

Architects should resist invitations to 'approve' the contractor's setting out. Provided that he is given adequate and accurate information, responsibility for accuracy rests with the contractor. Acceptance of errors in setting out is the employer's option and his instructions should be obtained in that event.

Volume 1
Fig K4.1 Specimen agenda for Architect's Progress Meeting
K5 Setting Out

JCT 80

Clause 7
The architect is responsible for determining the levels required for carrying out the works. He must provide accurately dimensioned drawings containing whatever information the contractor needs to set out the works at ground level.

Unless the architect instructs otherwise, the contractor is responsible for amending at his own cost any errors arising from inaccurate setting out.

The architect may instruct otherwise where the employer authorises him to accept the errors in return for an appropriate deduction from the contract sum.

The Approximate Quantities version has adapted wording for dealing with the ascertained final sum.

> The Architect shall determine any levels ... and shall provide the Contractor ... accurately dimensioned drawings ... as shall enable the Contractor to set out ... *(Clause 7)*

IFC 84

Clause 3·9

The provision is broadly similar to Clause 7 of JCT 80, but there is no mention of information being related to ground level. The contract sum may be adjusted if a contractor's error in setting out is accepted by the employer. An Architect's Instruction to this effect should only be issued after the employer's written consent has been obtained.

> The Architect shall determine any levels which may be required ... shall provide ... accurately dimensioned drawings ... as shall enable the Contractor to set out ... *(Clause 3·9)*

MW 80

There is no express provision dealing with setting out.

Fig 3.13.1

Specimen letter to contractor in reply to query about setting out

```
        Thank you for your letter of (date) querying the setting-out of
        the works and the fixing of levels.

        The setting-out information you need is given on drawing (no.)
        issued under Architect's Instruction (no.) of (date). The
        building line is related to the existing back of pavement line.

        With regard to your query about the bench-mark for the datum
        level of the works, we confirm that (name) will meet you on site
        at (time) on (date) to resolve this matter.



        Copy to: clerk of works
```

The role of the clerk of works is limited by the terms of the contract to that of inspector on behalf of the employer. Subject to the contract terms, the employer is entitled to appoint a clerk of works, and the contractor is obliged to allow him access.

The clerk of works is not usually empowered to issue instructions. If his duties are to be extended, they should be precisely defined and details included in the tender documents. These should also describe the accommodation, equipment and facilities which the contractor is required to provide for the clerk of works.

Where the architect is asked to advise on the appointment of a clerk of works, he should try to ensure that a suitable and competent person is engaged. The clerk of works should be employed direct by the employer. If the employer requires the clerk of works to be employed by the architect, the architect would be wise to obtain an indemnity from the employer.

The clerk of works is normally under the architect's direction and control. He should be fully briefed about his duties under the contract in question.

Volume 1
Action checklist
F2.1 (70)
J5 Clerk of Works

JCT 80

Clause 12

The employer is entitled to appoint a clerk of works, and the contractor is required to provide reasonable facilities for his duties to be carried out on site. The clerk of works is employed as an inspector under the direction of the architect, who is responsible for briefing and supervising him.

The clerk of works is authorised to issue directions to the contractor on those matters about which the architect is authorised to issue instructions. The directions of the clerk of works do not have effect until confirmed in writing by the architect.

The clerk of works' directions should be completed in triplicate. One copy is handed to the person-in-charge, one sent to the architect, and one kept by the clerk of works.

Although the contract requires for directions by the clerk of works to be confirmed by the architect within two working days of issue, the employer's or architect's organisations may well need a longer period, in which case other arrangements should be agreed at the outset.

When confirming directions by the clerk of works by Architect's Instruction, the date and number of the direction should be quoted and the same words used (and amplified if necessary).

If the architect does not wish to confirm a direction of the clerk of works he should notify the clerk of works and the contractor immediately.

> The employer shall be entitled to appoint a clerk of works ...
> if any direction is given ... by the clerk of works ... the same
> shall be of no effect ... unless confirmed in writing by the
> Architect within 2 working days ... *(Clause 12)*

IFC 84

Clause 3·10
The employer is entitled to appoint a clerk of works to act as inspector under the direction of the architect. There is no reference to the issue of directions by the clerk of works, so appropriate provisions would have to be incorporated as required.

> The Employer shall be entitled to appoint a clerk of works ...
> *(Clause 3·10)*

MW 80

There are no provisions concerning a clerk of works.

Fig 3.14.1

Specimen letter to contractor For use with JCT 80
concerning the appointment of a clerk of works

Much of the subject matter will be covered at the initial project meeting, but a letter on these lines may still be appropriate.

```
The new clerk of works (name), will begin duties on site at
(time) on (date). Site accommodation and attendance to be
provided are described in (item) on (page), and (item) on (page)
respectively of the Bills of Quantities. These provisions will be
required from the start date.

We enclose a statement of the clerk of works' duties and
authority, and our standard form of weekly report which he will
complete for our information. Your cooperation and that of your
staff in helping him to perform his duties will be appreciated.
```

The employer may wish to carry out work or have it carried out by others during the time that the contractor is in possession of the site.

Volume 1
J6 Initial Project Meeting

This requirement should be included in the tender documents where possible, and the contractor may be expected to have made appropriate allowances in his tender.

The work concerned should be carefully defined and the responsibilities in connection with it precisely specified.

Where the employer's intention to carry out such work is not known at the time of tender, the work can only be done during the contract with the contractor's agreement.

JCT 80

Clause 29·1

The contractor is required to permit the employer, or persons directly engaged by the employer, to carry out work not forming part of the contract. This is provided that the contract bills/specification contain sufficient information for the contractor to take account of the effects in his tender, and allow him to carry out and complete the works in accordance with the contract. Under these circumstances he has no right of objection.

Clause 29·2

Where the contractor was not made aware of work to be carried out by the employer or persons directly engaged by the employer at the time of tendering and there is no relevant information in the contract bills/specification, then such work requires the contractor's consent.

In the case of Clause 29·1 and particularly Clause 29·2, the scope and timing of the work, extent of liability and insurance arrangements should all be carefully defined.

> Where the Contract Bills ... provide such information as is necessary ... the Contractor shall permit the execution of such work. *(Clause 29·1)*
>
> Where the Contract Bills do not provide the information ... then the Employer may, with the consent of the Contractor ... arrange for the execution of such work. *(Clause 29·2)*

IFC 84

Clause 3·11

There is a provision broadly similar to Clause 29 of JCT 80. Work originally intended to be carried out by named persons as sub-contractors may also be carried out under this clause where a relevant Architect's Instruction is issued under Clause 3·3·1 or 3·3·4.

> Where the Contract Documents provide ... the Contractor shall permit the execution of such work on the site of the works ...
>
> Where the Contract Documents do not so provide the employer may ... with the consent of the contractor ... arrange for ... such work ... *(Clause 3·11)*

MW 80

There are no provisions for the employer to undertake work outside the contract.

Fig 3.15.1

Specimen letter to contractor requesting agreement to work being undertaken by the employer

For use with JCT 80

```
        The employer wishes to arrange for work which does not form part
        of the contract to be carried out between (date) and (date),
        subject to the following conditions:

        1    The employer's contractors will provide all materials, tools
             and labour, including off-loading and carrying.

        2    No power supply for tools and plant will be required, but
             artificial lighting will be needed.

        3    All waste materials and rubbish will be cleared by the
             employer's contractors.

        4    If any minor items of attendance or protection are needed
             during this work, they will be covered by an Architect's
             Instruction.

        The employer would be grateful to have your consent to this
        proposed work. Please advise us whether additional insurance will
        be required under clause 23.3 of the contract.



        Copy to: quantity surveyor
```

Volume 1
J6 Initial Project Meeting

Realistic provisional sums should be inserted in the bills of quantities or specification to cover the costs of routine and specific tests on materials and workmanship, including a certain amount of opening up to ensure that standards are in accordance with the contract.

The architect is empowered to require such testing and opening up. Loss resulting from work that fails to conform to the contract must be borne by the contractor. If the materials and workmanship prove to be satisfactory, then the cost is usually borne by the employer. If tests not provided for in the contract become advisable, the employer should be notified and alerted to the financial implications before instructions are issued.

The commissioning and testing of engineering installations is an important issue, and adequate time should be allowed within the contract period for this work. The tender documents should include a separate price for the provision of the required commissioning and testing procedures. The JCT forms of contract do not provide for this work to be undertaken after practical completion, and where it is necessary to do this after the building is occupied, special consideration should be given to the contractual arrangements. See NJCC *Procedure Note 15: 'Commissioning and Testing'*.

JCT 80

Clause 8·3

The architect may instruct the contractor to open up for inspection any work covered up. He may instruct the contractor to arrange or carry out tests on any executed work, materials or goods.

The contractor is required to produce evidence, at the architect's request, that goods and materials conform to the standards specified. The kinds of and standards for materials and goods, and standards of workmanship are referred to in Clause 8·1. The clerk of works should be briefed to obtain certificates, check delivery notes, examine goods for 'kite marks' etc as routine procedures.

If workmanship, goods or materials fail to comply with the standards of the contract, the contractor is to bear any loss. Otherwise, the expense arising from the opening up or tests is borne by the employer and, unless already provided for in the contract bills, added to the contract sum.

Clause 8·4

Where materials, goods or workmanship are found not to be in accordance with the contract, several courses of action are possible:
· the architect may order their removal from the site;
· the architect may – with the employer's agreement, and after consulting the contractor – allow the work or materials to remain. This must be confirmed in writing and a deduction calculated by the quantity surveyor, made from the contract sum;
· the architect may – after non-compliance has been discovered – order further testing or opening up. The architect must have regard to the Code of Practice* which is part of the contract and if the instruction is reasonable in this respect then the cost is borne by the contractor. However, if it is later discovered that the

work or materials did comply with the contract, then the contractor may be entitled to an extension of time.

> The Architect may issue instructions requiring the Contractor to open up for inspection ... or to arrange for or carry out any test ... *(Clause 8·3)*
>
> The Architect may ... issue instructions in regard to the removal from the site ... (1) ... allow all or any of such work, materials and goods to remain ... (2) ... issue such instructions requiring a variation as are reasonably necessary ... (3) ... issue such instructions under Clause 8·3 ... as are reasonable ... to establish ... further similar non-compliance ... (4). *(Clause 8·4)*

*Code of Practice referred to in Clause 8·4·4 (to be appended to 'The Conditions' after clause 37)

1   This is the Code of Practice referred to in clause 8·4·4. The purpose of the Code is to help in the fair and reasonable operation of the requirements of clause 8·4·4.

2   The Architect and the Contractor should endeavour to agree the amount and method of opening up or testing but in any case in issuing his instructions the Architect is required to consider the following criteria:

    ·1   the need in the event of non-compliance to demonstrate at no cost to the Employer either that it is unique and not likely to occur in similar elements of the Works or alternatively the extent of any similar non-compliance in the Works already constructed or still to be constructed;

    ·2   the need to discover whether any non-compliance in a primary structural element is a failure of workmanship and/or materials such that rigorous testing of similar elements must take place; or where the non-compliance is in a less significant element whether it is such as is to be statistically expected and can be simply repaired; or whether the non-compliance indicates an inherent weakness such as can only be found by selective testing the extent of which must depend upon the importance of any detail concerned;

    ·3   the significance of the non-compliance having regard to the nature of the work in which it has occurred;

    ·4   the consequence of any similar non-compliance on the safety of the building, its effect on users, adjoining property, and compliance with any Statutory Requirements;

    ·5   the level and standard of supervision and control of the Works by the Contractor;

·6   the relevant records of the Contractor and where relevant of any sub-contractor resulting from the supervision and control referred to in paragraph 2·5 above or otherwise;

·7   any Codes of Practice or similar advice issued by a responsible body which are applicable to the non-complying work, materials or goods;

·8   any failure by the Contractor to carry out, or to secure the carrying out of any tests specified in the Contract Documents or in an instruction of the Architect;

·9   the reason for the non-compliance when this has been established;

·10 any technical advice that the Contractor has obtained in respect of the non-complying work, materials or goods;

·11 current recognised testing procedures;

·12 the practicability of progressive testing in establishing whether any similar non-compliance is reasonably likely;

·13 if alternative testing methods are available, the time required for and the consequential costs of such alternative testing methods;

·14 any proposals of the Contractor;

·15 any other relevant matters.

IFC 84

Clause 3·12
Provisions are broadly similar to Clause 8·3 of JCT 80.

Clause 3·13
Where a failure of work or of materials and goods has been discovered, the contractor is responsible for taking action to establish that there is no similar failure in work already carried out, or in materials or goods already supplied. This is at no cost to the employer, regardless of the findings.

In certain (stated) circumstances, the architect may issue an instruction requiring the contractor to take certain action at no cost to the employer. There is a clear obligation to comply with this instruction. If the contractor disputes the instruction, the matter will automatically be referred to arbitration. If the arbitrator decides that the instruction was not fair and reasonable, he may award the contractor an extension of time and compensation for loss and expense incurred.

When considering matters of testing and the reasonableness of the
instructions, bear in mind the extent of the instruction. For example,
is the size of the selected batch reasonable? And does the test have
to test to destruction?

> The Architect may issue instructions requiring the Contractor
> to open up ... or to arrange for ... any test ... *(Clause 3·12)*
>
> If a failure ... is discovered ... the Contractor   ... shall state in
> writing ... the action which the Contractor will immediately
> take ... *(Clause 3·13·1)*.
>
> ... the Architect may issue instructions ... to establish that
> there is no similar failure ... The Contractor shall forthwith
> comply ... *(Clause 3·13·1)*

MW 80

There are no provisions concerning opening up or testing in the
conditions.

Issued by:
address:

Architect's instruction

Employer:
address:

Serial no:

Job reference:

Contractor:
address:

Issue date:

Contract dated:

Works:
Situated at:

Under the terms of the above Contract, I/We issue the following instructions:

	Office use: Approx costs	
	£ omit	£ add

OPENING-UP OF DRAIN FOR INSPECTION

Please open-up the drain connection manholes 2 and 3 for our
inspection and arrange for water pressure tests to be
carried out at (time) on (date) in the presence of the clerk
of works.

This instruction is issued in accordance with clause 8.3 of
the contract.

[Add copy to clerk of works]

To be signed by or for
the issuer named
above.   Signed _____

Amount of Contract Sum	£
± Approximate value of previous instructions	£ _____
	£
± Approximate value of this instruction	£ _____
Approximate adjusted total	£

Distribution   ☐ Employer   ☐ Contractor   ☐ Quantity Surveyor   ☐ Services Engineer

☐   ☐ Nominated   ☐ Structural Engineer   ☐ File
Sub-Contractors

© 1985 RIBA Publications Ltd

Fig 3.16.2　　　**Specimen AI accepting work not in accordance with the contract**　　　For use with JCT 80

Issued by:
address:

Architect's instruction

Employer:
address:

Serial no:

Job reference:

Contractor:
address:

Issue date:

Contract dated:

Works:
Situated at:

Under the terms of the above Contract, I/We issue the following instructions:

	Office use: Approx costs
	£ omit　　　│£ add

WORK NOT IN ACCORDANCE WITH THE CONTRACT

Following our discussion on site, and with the agreement of
the employer:

1　　You are instructed to leave the skirting brick wall
　　with the plinth set off as constructed. No deduction
　　from the contract sum is thought to be appropriate.

　　This instruction is issued under clause 8.4.2 of the
　　contract.

2　　As a direct consequence of allowing this wall to
　　remain, you are further instructed to:
　　(a)　amend the brackets for the sheeting rails as shown
　　　　on the attached drawing (no.);
　　(b)　amend the profile of the brick coping as shown on
　　　　the attached drawing (no.).

We confirm that these variations are at no cost to the
employer and that no extension of time will be given.

This instruction is issued under clause 8.4.3 of the
contract.

To be signed by or for
the issuer named
above.　　　　　**Signed** _____

Amount of Contract Sum　£
± Approximate value of previous instructions　£ _____
£
± Approximate value of this instruction　£ _____
Approximate adjusted total　£

Distribution　　☐ Employer　　☐ Contractor　　☐ Quantity Surveyor　　☐ Services Engineer

☐　　☐ Nominated
Sub-Contractors　　☐ Structural Engineer　　☐ File

© 1985 RIBA Publications Ltd

Fig 3.16.3   **Specimen AI concerning testing to establish any further non-compliance**   For use with JCT 80

Issued by:
address:

Employer:
address:

Contractor:
address:

Works:
Situated at:

Architect's instruction

Serial no:

Job reference:

Issue date:

Contract dated:

Under the terms of the above Contract, I/We issue the following instructions:

	Office use: Approx costs	
	£ omit	£ add

FURTHER OPENING-UP FOLLOWING DISCOVERY OF WORK NOT IN ACCORDANCE WITH CONTRACT

We refer to our discovery of the incorrectly placed lead damp-proof tray at the head of an oriel window yesterday.

You are instructed to open-up for our inspection the heads of five further oriel windows, as marked on the attached plan.

Having regard to the Code of Practice, we consider that this is the minimum sample necessary as a first stage investigation. It may be that opening-up can be achieved by removing internal blockwork, leaving the facing brick undisturbed, but this is a matter for you to decide.

This is to be at no cost to the employer.

This instruction is issued under clause 8.4.4 of the contract.

To be signed by or for
the issuer named
above.   Signed _____

Amount of Contract Sum	£
± Approximate value of previous instructions	£ _____
	£
± Approximate value of this instruction	£ _____
Approximate adjusted total	£

Distribution ☐ Employer   ☐ Contractor   ☐ Quantity Surveyor   ☐ Services Engineer

☐   ☐ Nominated   ☐ Structural Engineer   ☐ File
Sub-Contractors

© 1985 RIBA Publications Ltd

The contractor is obliged to carry out and complete the works to the standards specified in the contract otherwise, in the absence of anything to the contrary in the contract, he will be in breach of contract. Architects should make sure that defective work or materials are not included by the quantity surveyor in a valuation.

JCT forms have traditionally provided the architect with power to order the removal of any work, materials or goods not in accordance with the contract. This is not a declaration simply condemning work – the instruction must require removal from the site. The quantity surveyor should be notified.

JCT 80

Clause 8·4

The architect may issue instructions for the removal from site of any work, materials or goods which are not in accordance with the contract.

The Architect's Instruction should follow the wording of the clause precisely. 'Removal from site' is the operative requirement.

The quantity surveyor should be notified that such work, materials or goods should not be included in an interim valuation.

> ... the Architect ... may ... issue instructions in regard to the removal from the site ... *(Clause 8·4·1)*

IFC 84

Clause 3·14

There is a provision identical to Clause 8·4·1 of JCT 80.

> The Architect may issue instructions in regard to the removal from the site ... *(Clause 3·14)*

MW 80

There is no provision concerning the removal of work in the conditions.

Issued by:
address:

Employer:
address:

Contractor:
address:

Works:
Situated at:

Architect's instruction

Serial no:

Job reference:

Issue date:

Contract dated:

Under the terms of the above Contract, I/We issue the following instructions:

	Office use: Approx costs	
	£ omit	£ add
REMOVAL OF MATERIALS: ROOFING FELT You are instructed to remove from site all roofing felt bearing the name 'Tearaway'. This material does not conform to BS 757 Class 2 as specified. This instruction is issued in accordance with clause 8.4.1 of the contract.		

To be signed by or for
the issuer named
above.

Signed _____

Amount of Contract Sum	£
± Approximate value of previous instructions	£ _____
	£
± Approximate value of this instruction	£ _____
Approximate adjusted total	£

Distribution   ☐ Employer   ☐ Contractor   ☐ Quantity Surveyor   ☐ Services Engineer

☐   ☐ Nominated   ☐ Structural Engineer   ☐ File
Sub-Contractors

© 1985 RIBA Publications Ltd

Unless expressly provided for in the contract, the employer has no power to postpone any work.

JCT forms have traditionally empowered the architect to postpone any part or all of the work. This does not extend to an instruction purporting to postpone possession of the site.

If a postponement instruction is to be expressly issued, the employer should be advised about the financial and other implications if the delay is likely to be lengthy.

Notices should be carefully worded. For example, an Architect's Instruction which results in the contractor having to re-programme his work might be construed as a postponement instruction. So might a letter in which the architect apparently agrees with the contractor that a hold-up means that not much can usefully be done on site – even though this was not what he meant to convey.

JCT 80

Clause 23·2

The architect may issue instructions regarding the postponement of any work. This may be any part or even the whole of the works. It is not held to include postponing possession of the site.

Any direct loss or expense incurred by the contractor will be valued under Clause 26. If the delay exceeds the period stated in the Appendix, postponement will also provide valid grounds for determination by the contractor.

> The Architect may issue instructions in regard to ...
> postponement ... *(Clause 23·2)*

IFC 84

Clause 3·15

There is a provision identical to Clause 23·2 of JCT 80.

> The Architect may issue instructions in regard to ...
> postponement ... *(Clause 3·15)*

MW 80

There is no provision concerning postponement in these conditions

Issued by:
address:

Employer:
address:

Contractor:
address:

Works:
Situated at:

Architect's instruction

Serial no:

Job reference:

Issue date:

Contract dated:

Under the terms of the above Contract, I/We issue the following instructions:

| | Office use: Approx costs | |
| | £ omit | £ add |

POSTPONEMENT OF WORK

All work to the laundry block is to be suspended
immediately, pending an independent consultant's report on
the defective piling. Work may not be resumed on this block
until further notice.

The area should be made safe and secure through the period
of investigation.

This Instruction is issued in accordance with clause 23.2.

[Add copy to clerk of works]

To be signed by or for
the issuer named
above.   Signed _____

Amount of Contract Sum	£
± Approximate value of previous instructions	£ _____
	£
± Approximate value of this instruction	£ _____
Approximate adjusted total	£

Distribution   ☐ Employer   ☐ Contractor   ☐ Quantity Surveyor   ☐ Services Engineer

☐   ☐ Nominated   ☐ Structural Engineer   ☐ File
                Sub-Contractors

© 1985 RIBA Publications Ltd

Sub-contracting
* Check the written request from the contractor asking you to approve sub-contracting. It should:
  · refer to the contract clause;
  · identify precisely the extent of the work to be sub-contracted;
  · name the firm of sub-contractors proposed;
  · request written consent for the sub-contract.

Then make your own enquiries about the firm proposed.

Listed persons
* Where it is proposed to include a list of sub-contractors for use with MW 80 or IFC 84, follow closely the wording recommended in National Building Specification. With IFC 84 state that Clause 3·2 and **not** Clause 3·3 applies. Amendments to the contract must be written into the contract.

Listed persons under JCT 80
* Where a list of sub-contractors is proposed under JCT 80 Clause 19·3, check that firms are 'able and willing' before including names. Make sure that work is properly measured or described in the bills and that the full information on which the sub-contractor's price is to be based is sent to him. Make a careful record of these documents, in case changes are made later.

Naming under IFC 84
* Decide early on whether it is necessary to name sub-contractors and, if so, which Procedure is appropriate. Procedure 1 requires attention earlier, but is more certain in terms of price. Adopt it wherever possible.

* If Procedure 1 is adopted, obtain NAM/T with Sections 1 and 2 completed, and issue copies with tender documents to the contractor. Keep a check on the accuracy of particulars during lead time *before* the main contract is let. Make sure that numbered documents and priced documents have been obtained from the named person.

* If Procedure 2 is adopted, ensure that the provisional sum is realistic and that work which is to be the subject of named person provisions is clearly identified in the contract documents. (Some quantity surveyors require the contractor to state profit and attendance against the provisional sum, but the contract does not require this.) Make sure that NAM/T is properly completed and that the supporting documents have been prepared to accompany the Architect's Instruction. It is wise to consult the main contractor before issuing the instruction, to forestall possible objections.

Collateral agreements
* Recommend in writing that the employer enters into collateral agreements with specialist sub-contractors whenever an element of design is involved.

'Watchpoints'

Nomination procedures
When nominating sub-contractors under JCT 80:

* only nominate for a good reason and use the 'basic' method if possible, particularly where the integration of the sub-contractor's work programme is critical;

* make sure you fill in Schedule 1 of NSC/1 fully. Check carefully that Schedule 2 is complete in matters of programme periods, special attendance, and includes the name of the adjudicator/stakeholder. Beware of phrases such as 'to be agreed';

* check that NSC/2 is properly executed. Beware of any attempts to amend the terms or make the tender conditional. Only issue instructions ordering advance work where absolutely necessary, and advise the employer of the possible consequences;

* if you do nominate by the 'alternative' method, use the optional tender NSC/1a and instruction NSC/3a. And check that the sub-contractor's programme can be accommodated within the main contract *before* nominating;

* when you have to 'approve' the sub-contractor's drawings (wording used in NSC/1), do so via the main contractor. Restrict approval to those matters stated in 'Architect's Appointment' (ie coordination and integration into the overall design – Clause 3·8).

* check that the main contractor and the sub-contractor actually enter into NSC/4, and that there is a start and completion date for the sub-contract. If NSC/4a (with conditions incorporated by reference) is used, insist on being given a copy of the Appendix.

Running a job with nominated sub-contractors
When running a job with nominated sub-contractors:

* remember that the procedural rules governing nominated sub-contractors require complex administrative procedures. Read them carefully, and check that they are followed throughout the job. Ignore them at your peril!

Paying nominated sub-contractors
* Identify sums due to particular nominated sub-contractors under Interim Certificates, and direct the main contractor about payment. Inform each nominated sub-contractor.

* Check that the main contractor has paid nominated sub-contractors before issuing the next Interim Certificate. The main contractor is required to provide *the architect* with reasonable proof of discharge (not necessarily payment) *every time* sums for nominated sub-contractors are included. If he fails to do so without good reason, issue a certificate to that effect with a copy to the nominated sub-contractor involved. Direct payment procedures will be implemented once the certificate has been issued.

Extension of time

* If the nominated sub-contractor requests an extension of sub-contract time through the main contractor, you must make your decision within the time scale stipulated in the contract.

Failure to complete

* If the nominated sub-contractor fails to complete within the sub-contract period, wait for formal notification from the main contractor. Investigate the reasons thoroughly and make sure that no extension of time has been overlooked. Then, and only then, issue the Certificate of Non-completion, with a copy to the nominated sub-contractor.

Practical completion of sub-contract works

* Remember that notification of practical completion of nominated sub-contract works begins with the sub-contractor notifying the main contractor, who must notify the architect. Certify practical completion only when you are satisfied that it has been achieved. Copy the certificate to the nominated sub-contractor.

* Remember that, subject to the defects being made good, final payment to nominated sub-contractors must be made within 12 months of the date of practical completion of the sub-contract works.

* Any outstanding sums due to nominated sub-contractors must be covered by an Interim Certificate issued not less than 28 days before the issue of the Final Certificate for the works. This should alert them that the Final Certificate is imminent, and give them a last chance to check that no unresolved disputes concerning set-off remain. This is important, because the certificate is final where monetary matters are concerned.

* Work reserved to be done by nominated sub-contractors can only be done by them. Any further nomination should be made within a reasonable time. Make sure that it is valid; check that sub-contract and main contract programmes are compatible. If there is any need to remedy defective work by a defaulting nominated sub-contractor who cannot or will not return to site, this must be included under the terms of the new nomination.

Administrative procedures

* Establish firm administrative procedures at the outset. All instructions, including those from consultants, must be issued by you. Make sure that they are clear, unambiguous and in writing.

Opening up and testing

* You are empowered by the contract to have completed work opened up. Include an adequate provisional sum to cover testing. Always try to make your instructions fair and reasonable.

Site inspections

* Carry out all site inspections methodically and keep meticulous records.

Payment

4

References

JCT

Practice Notes
12: Direct Payment and Final Payment to Nominated
    Sub-contractors
17: Fluctuations
18: Payment and Retention

IN/1 (Fluctuations)

Fluctuations Clauses and Formula Rules
(for use with IFC 84)
Formula Rules
(for use with NAM/SC)

NJCC

Code of Procedure for Single Stage Tendering
(alternatives for dealing with errors in contractor's tender)
Procedure Note:
11 Financial Control and Cash Flow

RIBA

'Practice'
Final Certificate (June 1985 p5)
Contractors' Claims (April 1986 p7)

Contract Sum

In a lump sum contract the employer pays the contractor an agreed sum for the work to be done. This is usually stated to exclude VAT.

The sum may be adjusted either way (if the contract conditions provide for this) to accommodate provisional sums, variations, fluctuations, loss and/or expense claims and so on.

Subject to the contract provisions, the parties are normally bound by any errors or omissions which are only discovered after the contract was made and subsequently incorporated in the contract sum.

The contractor's tender will not become a contract sum until it is accepted as such. Thus any procedures operated to adjust the tender may result in the contract sum being different from the original tender figure. There is a model procedure for dealing with errors in a tender figure in the appropriate NJCC Code of Procedure.

JCT 80

The contract sum will be inserted in Article 2.

Clause 14
The contract sum may only be adjusted in accordance with the contract conditions. Errors in computation are deemed to have been accepted by the parties.

Clause 3
Where it is necessary to make adjustments to the contract sum, the additions or deductions will be taken into account in the next Interim Certificate.

IFC 84

The contract sum will be inserted in Article 2.

Clause 4·1
There is a similar provision to Clause 14 of JCT 80.

Clause 4·2
Adjustments made to the contract sum under specified clauses are to take effect in the next Interim Certificate.

MW 80

The sum will be inserted in Article 2.

There is no express reference to the contract sum, but the conditions provide for variations and provisional sums.

4.2   Progress Payments

Even under a 'lump sum' contract, it is normal practice to make payments to the contractor as the work proceeds. Cash flow is the life blood of the construction industry. The contractor may have to borrow money to enable operations to be carried out and interest charges, which may be heavy, will be a factor he will take into account when tendering.

Volume 1
J6 Initial Project Meeting

It is customary to agree periodic intervals for valuations and the issue of Interim Certificates, but if there are no express provisions the parties are free to adopt whatever procedures suit them best. This may affect the intervals for certification and the period required for payment after certification. They may prefer stage payments; if so, the stages need to be clearly defined at the outset. Whatever method is agreed, it is desirable that the employer knows the pattern of progress payments and the anticipated approximate sums, so that appropriate arrangements may be made for prompt payment.

Where a quantity surveyor is employed, valuations will normally coincide with the issue of certificates. The roles of quantity surveyor and architect are quite distinct, and the valuation figure will not necessarily be the same as the one on the Interim Certificate. It is sensible to set up a simple checking procedure to exclude from the valuation workmanship or materials known by the architect not to be in accordance with the contract.

Under the terms of the contract, the employer's obligation to pay is usually dependent on an architect's certificate. The architect as certifier has a duty not only to the employer but also to the contractor to remain independent and to make his decision free from coercion or pressure from either party.

JCT 80

Clause 30

The parties may agree to stage payments (Clause 30·2). Otherwise, Interim Certificates must be issued at the intervals stated in the Appendix (usually one month). The contractor is entitled to payment within 14 days from the date of issue. The architect should be sure that the employer is fully aware of this.

The amount shown on an Interim Certificate is the total value of work properly executed, together with the value of goods and materials properly delivered to, or adjacent to, the works (subject to the conditions of Clause 16) up to 7 days before the date of the certificate, less the total previously certified and any retention.

Any work not properly executed should be excluded. The following procedure is recommended. Before issuing any Interim Certificate, ask the quantity surveyor to confirm that the valuation excludes work which he has been informed is defective. At the start of the job, agree with the quantity surveyor a regular sequence of site inspection/measurement and valuation/report/certification procedures, so that there can be a regular exchange of information for the purposes of certifying.

The retention percentage is normally 5% (unless a lower figure is agreed as suggested in Clause 30·4·1·1). A statement of retention is to be issued at each Interim Certificate to the employer, the contractor and each nominated sub-contractor whose work is included. In the private edition, if the contractor or any nominated sub-contractor so requests, retention money must be placed in a separate bank account (Clause 30·5·3).

Materials or goods off-site may be included at the discretion of the architect. Make sure that the provisions of Clause 30·3 are complied with before certification and that such compliance continues.

The right of the employer to make deductions from monies due to the contractor is limited by the provisions of the contract. The employer is also required to inform the contractor in writing before doing this.

Clause 35·13

The contractor must be informed of the amounts included in a certificate which are due to nominated sub-contractors, who should also be informed by the architect. An 'Interim Certificate and Direction' should be accompanied by a 'Statement of Retention and of Nominated Sub-contractor's Values', and a 'Notification to Nominated Sub-contractors Concerning Amount Included in Certificates' issued at the same time.

The contractor must provide the architect with reasonable proof of discharge. If he is unable to do so, then subject to the provisions of Clause 35·13, the architect must issue a certificate stating the amount for which the contractor has failed to provide proof, and send a copy to the nominated sub-contractor concerned. The employer is then required to pay the sub-contractor direct, provided that monies are due to the contractor from which deductions may be made.

Clause 36
There is no provision for direct payment to nominated suppliers.
Goods and materials from nominated suppliers will not be identified
separately on Interim Certificates.

The Architect shall ... issue Interim Certificates stating the
amount due to the Contractor ... the Contractor shall be
entitled to payment ... within 14 days ... *(Clause 30·1·1·1)*

... The Employer is entitled to exercise any right under this
Contract of deduction from monies due to ... the Contractor...
(Clause 30·1·1·2)

Where the Employer exercises any right ... of deduction ... he
shall inform the Contractor in writing of the reason ...
(Clause 30·1·1·3)

Interim valuations shall be made by the Quantity Surveyor ...
(Clause 30·1·2)

Interim Certificates shall be issued at the period of Interim
Certificates specified ... up to ... the Certificate of Practical
Completion ... Thereafter ... as and when ... *(Clause 30·1·3)*

The amount stated as due ... shall be the gross valuation ...
less ... the retention ... and the total amount stated as due in
Interim Certificates previously issued ... *(Clause 30·2)*

The Architect shall ... direct the Contractor as to the amount
of each interim or final payment to Nominated Sub-
Contractors ... ... and forthwith inform each Nominated
Sub-Contractor ... *(Clause 35·13·1)*

Before the issue of each Interim Certificate ... the Contractor
shall provide the Architect with reasonable proof of the
discharge ... *(Clause 35·13·3)*

If the Contractor fails to provide reasonable proof ... the
Architect shall issue a certificate ... *(Clause 35·13·5·2)*

IFC 84

Clause 4·2

Unless the parties agree to stage payments, Interim Certificates must be issued at the intervals stated in the Appendix (usually one month). The contractor is entitled to payment within 14 days of the date of the certificate. The architect should be sure that the employer is aware of this, and the first certificate at least should be sent to the employer with a covering letter pointing this out.

The amount certified should be for the total value of work properly executed, the valuation of variations and provisional sums, fluctuations, plus the value of materials and goods properly delivered to the site and protected.

The percentage not included in interim payments is 5%, which reduces to $2\frac{1}{2}$% on the issue of the certificate which follows practical completion. The balance of the percentage is taken into account in the Final Certificate.

Interim Certificates should include 100% of the value of items specified in Clause 4·2·2. Note also that 100% deductions may be made under items specified in Clause 4·2·2. Because no percentage can be withheld on these items, a separate note must be made, and a separate total kept for this item and shown separately on each certificate.

The architect may also agree to include the value of materials and goods off-site, but be careful about this – the provisions in the contract to protect the employer's interests are limited.

Unless agreed otherwise, certificates are to be issued to the employer, with a copy to the contractor.

Subject to any agreement ... as to stage payments, the Architect shall, at intervals of one month ... certify the amount of interim payments ... *(Clause 4·2)*

Interim valuations shall be made by the Quantity Surveyor whenever the Architect considers them to be necessary ... *(Clause 4·2)*

MW 80

Clause 4·2

If the contractor requests it, certificates of progress payments must be issued at intervals of not less than 4 weeks from the date work begins. The contractor is entitled to payment within 14 days of the date of the certificate. The architect should be sure that the employer is aware of this.

The amount certified is for the value of work properly executed, the valuation of variations and provisional sums, and the value of goods and materials properly delivered to site and protected.

The retention is generally 5% unless otherwise agreed, which reduces to $2\frac{1}{2}\%$ on the issue of the certificate which follows practical completion. The balance of the retention is taken into account in the Final Certificate.

There is no provision for including for off-site goods and materials.

Although not an express requirement, it is recommended that certificates should be issued to the employer, with a copy at the same time to the contractor.

The Architect shall if requested ... at intervals of not less than four weeks ... certify progress payments ... *(Clause 4·2)*

... The Employer shall pay ... within 14 days of the date of the Certificate. *(Clause 4·2)*

Fig 4.2.1   Specimen letter to private sector employer   For use with JCT 80
concerning setting up a trust account for retention money

We enclose a letter from the contractor requesting that the
retention money should be placed in a separate bank account in
accordance with clause 30.5.3 of the contract.

We therefore suggest that you open an account designated as the
'(name of project) Retention Trust Account' and transfer all
retention money into it and pay in further amounts as they become
due under Interim Certificates.

This does not detract from your interest in the retention as
security for the proper performance of the contractor and
nominated sub-contractors. Your interest is described in clause
30.5.1, and we remind you that you are under no contractual
obligation to invest the money.

When you have made the appropriate arrangements, please let us
know the name of the bank, and the title and number of the
account.

Copy to: quantity surveyor

Fig 4.2.2   Specimen letter to quantity surveyor   For use with JCT 80,
concerning the exclusion of unsatisfactory work and   IFC 84
materials from valuations

Before you prepare the next monthly valuation, please note our
Architect's Instruction (no.) of (date), concerning items of
unsatisfactory work and materials.

The items referred to should not be included in your valuation.

Copy to: consultant, clerk of works

Fig 4.2.3   **Specimen letter to contractor notifying direct certification**   For use with JCT 80

```
As you have failed to provide us with reasonable proof of payment
to the nominated sub-contractor (name), as included in our
Interim Certificate (no.) of (date), or have offered an
acceptable explanation for this omission, we are certifying
direct payment to them. This sum will be deducted from amounts
due to you in the next certificate.

This action is taken in accordance with clause 35.13.5 of the
contract.



Copy to: employer, quantity surveyor, consultant
```

Fig 4.2.4   **Specimen letter to employer certifying a direct payment to a nominated sub-contractor**   For use with JCT 80

```
The contractor has failed to provide reasonable proof of payment
of the sum of £ ..... due to the nominated sub-contractor (name)
under our Interim Certificate (no.) of (date), and has failed to
provide an acceptable explanation for non-payment.

Under clause 35.13.5.3 of the contract, and in accordance with
the terms of NSC/2, you are required to pay this sum direct. Your
interests are safeguarded however, because this sum will be
deducted from money otherwise due to the main contractor under
the next Interim Certificate.



Copy to: quantity surveyor, consultant
```

Fig 4.2.5   Specimen letter to nominated sub-contractor   For use with JCT 80
                             certifying a direct payment

We enclose a copy of a letter sent to the employer certifying
payment to you of the sum of £ ....., the sum due to you under
our Interim Certificate (no.) of (date).

This payment is certified in accordance with Clause 35.13.5 of
the contract, and Agreement NSC/2.

Please acknowledge receipt of payment to the employer direct.

Copy to: quantity surveyor, consultant

A 'fluctuating price' contract is one which allows the contract sum to be adjusted in line with increases or decreases in the cost of materials, labour and plant while the works are in progress.

Volume 1
J6 Initial Project Meeting
Action Checklist K2.1 (70)

Fluctuations can be dealt with in two ways:

(a)   *By a 'full fluctuations' recovery*
The quantity surveyor ascertains the actual fluctuations in price to the contractor by meticulously checking his vouchers and invoices. This method has been much criticised by contractors who maintain that reimbursement often falls short. The introduction of 'percentage additions' was an attempt to fend off this criticism.

(b)   *By adopting a formula*
Here the fluctuations are calculated theoretically, by reference to a set of indices. This is the more modern and, it is claimed, fairer method. In the case of JCT contracts, this method is based on the NEDO Price Adjustment Formula for Building Contracts, where the rules use indices compiled by the Department of the Environment and published monthly by HMSO.

Unless the conditions include a 'freezing provision', fluctuations may be payable for the whole time that the contractor is on site – even in the event of his failure to complete by the completion date.

JCT 80

Clause 37
The alternatives are listed and the choice should be entered in the Appendix. If there is no entry, then tax etc only fluctuations are to apply. The actual clauses are published separately.

Choices under JCT 80 are for:

(a) *Clause 38:* tax etc only;
(b) *Clause 39:* traditional full fluctuations on labour and materials costs;
(c) *Clause 40:* price adjustment formulae.

All have a freezing provision, but it only becomes operational if the Clause 25 text remains unamended and the extension of time procedures are meticulously followed by the architect.

Sums payable are added to the contract sum. Those in the case of Clause 40 only are subject to a retention.

IFC 84

Clause 4·9
The alternatives are listed, and the choice of formulae fluctuations can only apply if bills of quantities are a contract document. The actual clauses are supplemental conditions.

The choices under IFC 84 are:

(c) *Clause 4·9(a):* tax etc only;
(d) *Clause 4·9(b):* use of price adjustment formulae.

Sums payable are added to the contract sum. Formulae adjustment sums are subject to retention.

Note the particular provision in Clause 4·10 concerning fluctuations affecting named persons as sub-contractors.

MW 80

Clause 4·5
Fluctuations are limited to tax etc only – as in Part A of the Supplemental Memorandum. Even this provision may be deleted if appropriate for a particularly short contract period.

Volume 1
J6 Initial Project Meeting
Action checklist K2.1 (70)

The contractor may suffer loss and expense if regular progress of the works is not as he anticipated at the time he tendered. If this is the result of some action by the employer, then he is likely to claim compensation.

The contract may have express terms which provide a procedure for loss and expense to be ascertained and certified, but if it is silent and has no machinery for dealing with such matters the contractor can bring a common law claim for damages. This must be pursued by means of arbitration or litigation.

Direct loss should be distinguished from consequential loss, which is loss which does not result directly and naturally from the event. Heads of typical direct loss and expense might include site overheads, head office overheads, loss of profit, loss of productivity and interest or financing charges. The contractors' costs in preparing this information, unless an unusual format or amount of detail has been required by the architect, are not usually admissible.

The claimant also has an implied duty to mitigate his loss. For example, if the contractor's application was later than it should have been, and if by better deployment of men and equipment at the time, the impact could have been softened, then clearly the contractor has failed to mitigate his loss.

Extensions of time may, although not necessarily, give rise to applications for disturbance costs. Delay and disturbance are two distinct matters and should be considered separately.

JCT 80

Clause 26

If the contractor wishes to recover under this clause, he must apply in writing to the architect and show that he has incurred or is likely to incur direct loss and/or expense not otherwise recoverable under the contract.

The application must show that regular progress of the works or part of the works has been, or is likely to be affected by one or more of the matters listed in Clause 26·2.

The architect must decide whether or not regular progress has been materially affected. If he decides that it has, then the amount of the loss must be ascertained. This may be done by the architect, or by the quantity surveyor if instructed by the architect.

The contractor must provide the architect upon request with whatever information he needs to form an opinion. Similarly, he must, if requested, provide the architect or the quantity surveyor with details which are 'reasonably necessary' for the ascertainment.

Extensions of time given under Clause 25 will not necessarily result in payment under Clause 26; the issues are not necessarily connected. But if there is a connection, Clause 26·3 requires the architect to state it in writing.

Sums ascertained are to be added to the contract sum and included in the next Interim Certificate.

> The Contractor's application shall be made as soon as it has become, or should reasonably have become, apparent ... that the regular progress ... has been or was likely to be affected ... *(Clause 26·1·1)*
>
> The Contractor shall ... submit to the Architect upon request such information as should reasonably enable the Architect to form an opinion ... *(Clause 26·1·2)*
>
> The Contractor shall submit ... such details ... as are reasonably necessary ... *(Clause 26·1·3)*
>
> The Architect ... shall ascertain, or shall instruct the Quantity Surveyor to ascertain, the amount of such loss and/or expense ... *(Clause 26·1)*

IFC 84

Clause 4·11
The provisions are broadly similar to those in JCT 80 Clause 26.

The application must show that the contractor has incurred, or is likely to incur, direct loss and/or expense not recoverable otherwise under the contract due to

(a) *Clause 2·2:* deferment of possession of the site;
(b) *Clause 4·12:* regular progress being materially affected by one or more of the matters listed in the clause.

Sums ascertained are to be added to the contract sum and included in the next Interim Certificate.

> If ... the Architect is of the opinion that the Contractor has incurred or is likely to incur direct loss and/or expense ... then the Architect shall ascertain, or shall instruct the Quantity Surveyor to ascertain such loss and expense incurred ... *(Clause 4·11)*
>
> ... the Contractor shall ... submit such information ... as is reasonably necessary ... *(Clause 4·11)*

MW 80

There are no provisions for certifying direct loss and/or expense in the contract conditions, nor are the provisions for valuing and certifying variations and provisional sum work defined in as much detail as JCT 80 and IFC 84.

Depending on the circumstances, the inclusion of some provision in the contract documents may be advisable.

When practical completion is achieved it is usual, subject to the conditions of the contract, to release half the retention money. The contract sum, as finally adjusted, will often not be known at this stage.

Volume 1
Action checklist L2.1 (70)

Depending on the circumstances, and as the financial position becomes clearer, it might be fair to release further sums, although Interim Certificates will usually continue to be issued at the agreed intervals.

The architect should not attempt to deduct liquidated damages from amounts certified. Even if the employer seems to be entitled to such damages, he must still follow the procedures set out in the contract.

Some JCT contracts expressly require certificates to be issued within a stated period following practical completion.

JCT 80

Clause 30
Interim Certificates are required to be issued following practical completion as and when further amounts payable are ascertained, but not at intervals more frequent than monthly (except for Clause 30·7 below).

Not less than 28 days before the date of issue of the Final Certificate, and even though a period of one month may not have elapsed since the issue of any previous certificate, the architect is required to issue an Interim Certificate which includes all sums due to the nominated sub-contractor (Clause 30·7).

> ... not less than 28 days before the date of issue of the Final Certificate ... the Architect shall issue an Interim Certificate ... which shall include the amounts of the sub-contract sums for all Nominated Sub-Contracts ... *(Clause 30·7)*
>
> ... at any time after the day named in the Certificate issued under clause 35·16 the Architect may, and on the expiry of 12 months ... shall, issue an Interim Certificate ... which shall include the ... Final Sub-Contract Sum as finally adjusted ... provided always that the Nominated Sub-Contractor has remedied any defects ... and has sent through the Contractor ... all documents necessary for the final adjustment ... *(Clause 35·17).*

IFC 84

Clause 4·3

Within 14 days after the date of practical completion, the architect is required to issue an Interim Certificate. The amount of the percentage withheld by the employer is reduced to $2\frac{1}{2}$%.

The relatively short timescale means that the quantity surveyor must make his preparations in good time. It also requires cooperation on the part of the contractor.

> The Architect shall, within 14 days after the date of Practical Completion, certify payment ... to the Contractor ...
> *(Clause 4·3)*

MW 80

Clause 4·3

Within 14 days after the date of practical completion, the architect is required to issue a penultimate certificate. The amount of the percentage of retention is reduced to $2\frac{1}{2}$%.

> The Architect shall within 14 days after the date of Practical Completion ... certify payment to the Contractor ...
> *(Clause 4·3)*

After defects scheduled at the end of the defects liability period have been made good by the contractor and the final contract figure is known, the architect is required to issue the Final Certificate.

A final account is drawn up, showing what amounts are to be deducted from or added to the contract sum. The quantity surveyor and the contractor will have an opportunity to discuss this. Contract forms usually stipulate a date from practical completion by which the process of finalising measurement and valuation is to be completed.

The Final Certificate should not be issued before the defects have been made good (or some authorised financial settlement in lieu has been agreed between the parties) and the final contract figure ascertained. Its conclusiveness and the extent to which it may be reviewed by an arbitrator will depend on the wording of the contract.

Volume 1
Action checklist L2.1 (70)
L6 Final Account

JCT 80

Clause 30·8

The architect is required to issue a Final Certificate (and there is only one issued for each project, even though practical completion has been certified for each nominated sub-contract) not later than two months after whichever of the three following events occurs last:
·   the end of the defects liability period;
·   the date of issue of the Certificate of Making Good Defects;
·   the date on which the contractor was sent a statement of all adjustments to the contract sum and ascertainment of loss and/or expense.

In order that the latter can be produced (normally by the quantity surveyor) the contractor is obliged to supply all documents necessary (and this includes those which relate to nominated sub-contractors and suppliers) not later than six months after practical completion of the works (Clause 30·6).

The Final Certificate must state:
(a)   the sum of the amounts already certified in previous certificates;
(b)   the adjusted contract sum (ie the final sum).

The difference is the balance due to the contractor from the employer or (exceptionally) vice versa. The balance is payable within 28 days after the date of the certificate.

Clause 30·9

The Final Certificate is stated to be conclusive in respect of all monetary matters, except for instances of fraud, accidental inclusion or exclusion of the cost of work or materials, and arithmetical error. The certificate is not conclusive in financial matters over which the parties are not in agreement and about which they have initiated arbitration or legal proceedings.

The Final Certificate is conclusive on matters concerning extensions of time and amounts under Clause 26 for loss and/or expense.

The Final Certificate is conclusive evidence of the reasonable satisfaction of the architect in respect of materials and workmanship only where his approval was expressly required (under Clause 2·1). No approval should have been given which implies acceptance of latent defects. If latent defects have become apparent after practical completion which have not been made good, legal advice may be necessary before the Final Certificate is issued.

> ... the Architect shall issue the Final Certificate and inform each Nominated Sub-Contractor ... *(Clause 30·8)*

IFC 84

Clause 4·6

The architect is required to issue the Final Certificate within 28 days of sending the contractor the computation of the adjusted contract sum, or within 28 days of certifying completion of making good defects, whichever is the later.

The Final Certificate must state:
(a)   the sum of the amounts already certified;
(b)   the adjusted contract sum.

The amount certified is the amount due to the contractor from the employer or (exceptionally) vice versa. Subject to any amounts properly deductible by the employer, the balance is payable within 21 days of the date of the certificate.

Clause 4·7

Unless proceedings to commence arbitration or litigation have been commenced within 21 days of the date of the certificate, the Final Certificate is conclusive as a certificate for payment, except in respect of accidental inclusion or exclusion of any item and any arithmetical error.

> The Architect shall, within 28 days of the sending of ... the adjusted Contract Sum ... or of a Certificate issued by the Architect under clause 2·10 (Defects Liability) whichever is the later, issue a Final Certificate ... *(Clause 4·6)*

MW 80

Clause 4·4

The contractor is obliged to supply all documentation reasonably required for the computation of the amount finally to be certified within three months from the date of practical completion. The architect is obliged to issue the Final Certificate within 28 days of the receipt of this documentation, provided that the architect has issued a certificate under Clause 2·5.

The Final Certificate is solely a monetary certificate. It must show the balance due to the contractor by the employer or (exceptionally) vice versa. Payment is to be made from the 14th day after the date of the certificate.

> ... and the Architect shall within 28 days of receipt of such documentation, provided that the Architect has issued the Certificate under clause 2·5 hereof, issue a Final Certificate ... *(Clause 4·4)*

'Watchpoints'

Timescale for payments

* Check that the intervals between issuing Interim Certificates and the timescale for payment is in line with the employer's financial capability. The employer must be made aware of the financial commitments before he enters into a contract and must be sure that he has the resources to meet them. He should if necessary be provided with an approximate expenditure forecast (with sensible contingencies) and this may need updating from time to time. If difficulties are anticipated, this must be made clear at tender stage and adjustments made to resolve the problem.

Retention pending audit

* If money is to be held back by the employer pending audit, this also must be made clear at tender stage. But it should be noted that JCT contracts do not recognise this practice, and the audit should not be allowed to hamper your duty to certify.

Certifying

* Don't blindly accept the quantity surveyor's valuation as the figure to be certified. Agree a checking procedure to avoid the risk of unacceptable work being included in valuations. Remember *you* are responsible for issuing certificates.

Off-site goods and materials

* Do not include off-site goods and materials in certificates without very good reasons, and then take great care to check that the items are properly identified, protected and insured. Check again before issuing each subsequent certificate and obtain the employer's authority. Beware of attempts to use this provision to obtain payment for goods purchased long before they are required.

Nominated sub-contractors

* Where there are nominated sub-contractors, make sure that the contractor supplies proof of discharge before you issue the next certificate. It is his duty to supply you (not the quqntity surveyor) with this. Check that all outstanding matters with nominated sub-contractors have been cleared before you issue the Final Certificate.

Liquidated damages

* Do not deduct liquidated damages. This is solely a matter for the employer. Remind him that his opportunity to recover damages ceases after the Final Certificate.

Final Certificate

* Do not issue the Final Certificate if you have reason not to be satisfied that the works are free from defects for which the contractor is responsible.

Delay v. disturbance

* Do not confuse matters concerning notice of delay (time-related to the contract completion date) with applications for reimbursement of direct loss and expense (money-related to disturbance of regular progress). Extensions of time do not automatically entail financial compensation.

Loss and expense for disturbance

* It is your duty to reach an opinion on a written application for loss and expense and to give instructions for it to be ascertained. The regular progress of work must be materially affected by one or more of the specified matters. A written application from the contractor is required.

Statutory Obligations 5

References

JCT

Practice Notes
6:    Value Added Tax
8:    Statutory Tax Deduction Scheme

RIBA

'Practice'
VAT on Infill (June 1984 pp 1, 7)
Conditional Passing of Plans (April 1985 p2)
VAT Listed Buildings (May 1985 p7)
Provisions for 'Fair Wages' (September 1985 p2)
VAT News (June 1986 p2)
Building Regulations (February 1987 p3)
Building Regulations (April 1987 p3)
Building Regulations (August 1987 p9)
Model Water Byelaws (August 1987 p4)
Health & Safety at Work Act 1974 (September 1987 p10)
Stop Notices Reviewed (October 1987 p3)
Building (Disabled People) Regulations 1987 (November 1987 p1)
Building Regulations (April 1988 p5)
Building Control (May 1988 p7)

Compliance with Statutory Requirements

The contract conditions may reinforce the statutory duty of the contractor to comply with certain statutory requirements relating to building works and site operations. These include the *Public Health Act 1961*, the *Defective Premises Act 1972*, the *Health and Safety at Work etc Act 1974*, the *Occupiers Liability Act 1984*, the *Building Act 1984*, and regulations arising from them. Compliance with Acts of Parliament, Statutory Instruments, Regulations and Byelaws is an obligation notwithstanding the express terms of a building contract.

Under certain circumstances the employer could be held liable for works that do not conform to statutory requirements. Although the contractor is given possession of the site for the purposes of the contract, the employer as owner of the site still has legal obligations. The contractor's responsibility for conformity might in any case be reduced, once he has notified the employer via the architect that there are divergences between statutory requirements and the contract documents.

As soon as the contractor has performed his duty to point out divergences between statutory requirements and contract documents then the architect, on behalf of the employer, must issue instructions to clarify the situation.

JCT 80

Clause 6·1

The contractor must comply with, and give all notices required by any Act of Parliament or any regulations or byelaws of a local authority or statutory undertaker who has any jurisdiction over the works. But in accordance with Clause 6·1·5, conformity with the contract documents and the architect's instructions may entitle the contractor to be exonerated from liability to the employer, provided that the contractor has notified the architect of any divergence.

The contractor must immediately notify the architect in writing if a divergence is found, and the architect must issue instructions within 7 days of the discovery of the divergence or of receiving notification. If the instructions vary the works, then this is deemed to be a variation instruction issued under Clause 13·2.

The contractor is authorised to take emergency action to secure immediate compliance with statutory requirements, but this applies to essential work only, and subject to the architect being informed forthwith. Such action is to be treated as a deemed variation.

Clause 6·2

The contractor is obliged to pay all statutory fees or charges, and to indemnify the employer against liability. Unless these amounts are provisional sums, or are otherwise included in the contract or arise in connection with nominated sub-contractors or suppliers, they must be added to the contract sum.

... The Contractor shall comply with, and give all notices required by, any Act of Parliament, any instrument, rule or order made under Act of Parliament ... *(Clause 6·1·1)*

If the Contractor shall find any divergence ... he shall immediately give to the Architect a written notice ... *(Clause 6·1·2)*

If the Contractor gives notice ... the Architect shall within 7 days ... issue instructions ... *(Clause 6·1·3)*

The Contractor shall pay ... fees or charges ... legally demandable ... The amount ... shall be added to the Contract Sum ... *(Clause 6·2)*

IFC 84

Clauses 5·1 to 5·4

These provisions are similar to Clauses 6·1 and 6·2 of JCT 80. The contractor must comply with, and give all notices required by any Act of Parliament or any statutory instrument or byelaw. The contractor is obliged to pay all fees and charges, and these amounts are to be added to the contract sum.

If the contractor finds a divergence between the statutory requirements and the contractual obligations, he must immediately notify the architect in writing. Provided that he gives such notice, he is not liable to the employer under the contract if the works carried out under it do not comply with the statutes (Clause 5·3).

The contractor is authorised to take emergency action to secure immediate compliance with statutory requirements in the case of essential work only, and subject to the architect being informed forthwith. Such action is held to be a deemed variation.

The Contractor shall comply with, and give all notices required by, any statute ... *(Clause 5·1)*

If the Contractor finds any divergence ... he shall immediately give to the Architect a written notice ... *(Clause 5·2)*

MW 80

Clause 5·1

The contractor must comply with statutory requirements and pay all related fees and charges. If he finds divergences between the statutory requirements and the contract documents or the architect's instructions, he must immediately notify the architect in writing.

> The Contractor shall comply with, and give all notice required by, any statute ... *(Clause 5·1)*
>
> ... If the Contractor finds any divergence ... he shall immediately give to the Architect a written notice ... *(Clause 5·1)*

Fig 5.1.1   Specimen AI concerning a divergence between statutory requirements and contract documents   For use with JCT 80

Issued by: address:	**Architect's instruction**
Employer: address:	Serial no:
	Job reference:
Contractor: address:	Issue date:
	Contract dated:
Works: Situated at:	

Under the terms of the above Contract, I/We issue the following instructions:

	Office use: Approx costs	
	£ omit	£ add

AMENDMENT TO CONFORM WITH STATUTORY REQUIREMENTS:
Provision of Fire Doors

    OMIT (item) on (page) of the Bills of Quantities and as
    shown on our drawing (title, no.).

    ADD Fire Doors as shown on our drawing (title, no.).

This Instruction is issued in accordance with clause 6.1 of
the contract, and refers to your letter (ref.) of (date)
concerning requirements stated by the Fire Officer.

To be signed by or for the issuer named above.

Signed _____

Amount of Contract Sum	£	
± Approximate value of previous instructions	£	_____
	£	
± Approximate value of this instruction	£	_____
Approximate adjusted total	£	

Distribution

☐ Employer ☐ Contractor ☐ Quantity Surveyor ☐ Services Engineer

☐ ☐ Nominated Sub-Contractors ☐ Structural Engineer ☐ File

© 1985 RIBA Publications Ltd

Value Added Tax

VAT was introduced by the *Finance Act 1972* and its application was subsequently extended.

Work carried out under a building contract is a taxable supply of goods and services; the contractor has to pay whatever rate of VAT is applicable under current legislation. The way the tax is levied and the amounts payable are subject to constant change, and architects must always check the latest situation for themselves. There can be complications where part of the work is zero-rated and part is positively rated.

The contract sum is usually stated as excluding VAT.

When issuing certificates, the architect is not concerned with certifying liabilty for reimbursement of VAT. This is a separate matter between the contractor and the employer, although it is usual for the contractor to make a provisional assessment of the amount certified on which VAT will be chargeable. The contractual right to recover VAT is dealt with in a separate VAT Agreement or supplemental conditions.

JCT 80

Clause 15

This clause incorporates Supplemental Provisions. The contract sum is stated to exclude VAT, but it would be wise, when tenders are being considered, to give the employer some idea of the amount likely to be levied.

The architect should ask the contractor to notify the amount of VAT in an Interim Certificate, so that he may inform the employer. The employer will then remit this amount direct to the contractor.

Refer to JCT *Practice Note 6* for a detailed explanation of VAT and how it affects liquidated damages, nominated sub-contractors and suppliers, variations, provisional sum work and fluctuations.

> The Contractor shall not later than the date for ... each Interim Certificate ... give to the Employer a written provisional assessment ... of those supplies of goods and services ... which will be chargeable ... *(Supplemental Provisions, Clause 1·1)*
>
> After the issue of the Certificate of Completion of Making Good Defects ... the Contractor shall ... prepare a written final statement of the respective values of all supplies of goods and services ... which are chargeable ... *(Supplemental Provisions, Clause 1·3·1)*

IFC 84

Clause 5·5

This clause incorporates Supplemental Conditions A. The provisions are broadly similar to those under Clause 15 of JCT 80.

> The Contractor shall not later than ... each certificate of interim payment and ... the final certificate for payment give to the Employer a written provisional assessment ... *(Supplemental Condition A2)*

MW 80

Clause 5·2

This clause incorporates Part B of the Supplementary Memorandum. The provisions are broadly similar to those under Clause 15 of JCT 80.

> ... the Employer shall pay to the Contractor any value added tax properly chargeable ... *(Clause 5·2)*
>
> The Architect shall inform the Contractor of the amount certified ... the Contractor shall give to the Employer a written provisional assessment ... *(Supplementary Memorandum B2·1)*
>
> After the ... Certificate of Making Good Defects ... the Contractor shall ... submit to the Employer a written final statement ... *(Supplementary Memorandum B3·1)*

Volume 1
J6 Initial Project Meeting

The *Finance (No 2) Act 1975* was introduced to combat tax evasion in connection with labour-only sub-contracts. It is not concerned with payment for materials, but with sums which should be paid to the Inland Revenue such as income tax, corporation tax, and National Insurance contributions. In certain circumstances the employer in effect operates on behalf of the Inland Revenue and collects the tax.

Under the Act the employer may be classed as a 'contractor' and the main contractor a 'sub-contractor'. The main contractor will have to provide the employer with evidence that he holds a 'Sub-Contractor's Tax Certificate', if he claims that he should be paid in full. Three types of certificate are issued by the Inland Revenue.

The Statutory Tax Deduction Scheme operates quite apart from any contract provisions. Nevertheless JCT contracts provide for the orderly implementation of the scheme, and afford certain remedies and protection for the parties not available under the legisation.

JCT 80

Clause 31

It is essential for tenderers to know whether the employer is a 'contractor' within the meaning of the Act. This should be evident from the Fourth Recital and the appropriate deletion in the Appendix.

If the employer is a 'contractor', then the main contractor will need to satisfy him that he possesses a valid tax certificate. He can then be paid under certificates without any statutory deduction. It is unlikely that a main contractor who cannot produce a tax certificate will enter into a contract with an employer who is classed as a 'contractor'.

See JCT *Practice Note 8* for a detailed explanation of how the scheme is implemented.

> ... if, at any time up to the issue and payment of the Final Certificate, the Employer becomes such a 'contractor', the Employer shall so inform the Contractor ... *(Clause 31·2·2)*
>
> Not later than 21 days before the first payment ... is due ... the Contractor shall: provide ... evidence that the Contractor is entitled to be paid without statutory deduction; or inform the Employer ... that he is not entitled to be paid without the statutory deduction. *(Clause 31·3·1)*

IFC 84

Clause 5·6

This clause incorporates Supplemental Condition B. The provisions are similar to those under Clause 31 of JCT 80.

MW 80

Clause 5·3

This clause incorporates Part C of the Supplementary Memorandum. The provisions are similar to those under Clause 31 of JCT 80.

5.4   Fair Wages

The *Fair Wages Resolution* adopted by the House of Commons in 1946 was withdrawn in 1983. Any reference to the Minister of Labour or other government Ministers on questions in connection with fair wages thereupon ceased to be appropriate.

In addition, some local authorities have had a requirement concerning fair wages in Standing Orders, and some public bodies extended the provisions of a fair wages policy to cover other aspects of contractors' business, such as overseas connections, employment policy and working procedures. Such practices are now likely to be outside the law, particularly since the *Local Government Act 1988*. If any conditions of this kind, which are thought to be onerous, are inserted into the contract by local authority contract compliance units, they should immediately be referred to the NJCC for comment.

JCT 80

Clause 19A (Local Authorities Edition only)
The contractor is required to conform to local employment conditions to allow employees to belong to trade unions, to make records of wages and time sheets available to the employer, and to notify all employees of this clause.

The employer may require proof of this conformity in the execution of the works by the contractor and sub-contractors. Failure to comply with clause 19A is grounds for the employer to determine their employment.

> The Contractor shall pay rates of wages and observe hours and conditions of labour not less favourable than those established ... in the district ... *(Clause 19A·1·1)*

IFC 84

Clause 5·7 (only applies where the employer is a local authority)
This clause incorporates Supplemental Condition E. The provisions are broadly those under Clause 19A of JCT 80.

MW 80

Clause 5·4 (only applies where the employer is a local authority)
This clause requires compliance with the conditions of the fair wages provisions. Amendment MW1/1985 removes reference to the Fair Wages Resolution and substitutes a new Part D to the Supplementary Memorandum.

'Watchpoints'

Planning permission

* Before the contract is made, check that the planning permission which you obtained is still valid and not time-expired. However reluctant planning authorities might appear to be in taking enforcement actions, they still have the power to do so.

Compliance with Building Regulations

* The contractor has a clear duty to comply with the Building Regulations. If he queries whether your design complies in certain matters, check it out carefully. Remember that if you then instruct him to proceed in spite of having expressed doubts, you may carry some liability.

Environmental concerns

* Legislation covers many matters which can suddenly affect progress on site. For example, the *Wildlife and Countryside Act 1981* has in several reported cases caused work to be brought to a standstill whilst the welfare of protected species such as badgers or bats was resolved. Be alert about such matters – quite apart from the likelihood of delays, there are heavy fines.

Injury, Damage and Insurance 6

'Watchpoints'

References

JCT

Practice Notes
22 (and Guide to Amendments 1986)
Note: Practice Notes 2 and 3 apply only to forms without the 1986 amendments to the Insurance and Related Liability Provisions and are withdrawn.

RIBA

'Practice'
Making sure the contractor is adequately insured (July 1985 p7)*
Administering IFC 84 clause 6.2.4 (August 1985 p1)*
Employers' existing premises (October 1985 p 7)*
Meaning of 'sole risk' (December 1985 p1)*
The dangers of use or occupation (January 1986 p2)*
Meaning of 'All risks' (May 1986 p1)*
Pitfalls in contractors' insurances (June 1986 p1)*
'At the sole risk' (September 1986 p1)*
Amendments to JCT insurance provisions (December 1986 p 3)
Employer's loss of liquidated damages (March 1987 p7)
Alterations to buildings (September 1987 p4)
Insuring existing retained structures (October 1987 p 1)

*Contract refers to situation before the 1986 insurance and related liability amendments.

A Guide to Indemnity and Insurance
by Peter Madge
(Chapters 4,5,8,10,11)
1985 RIBA Publications

A Concise Guide to the 1986 Insurance Clauses
by Peter Madge
1987 RIBA Publications

Building sites are dangerous places, and substantial claims often arise in respect of personal injury or death. Claims for damage to property can be even more costly. The contractor may be mainly liable for such matters, but the employer cannot escape all liability by simply contending that the contractor is in possession of the site.

The employer can be protected from claims in the first place through indemnities given by the contractor, but these are worthless unless they are backed up by adequate resources. This usually means that the contractor has to arrange insurance cover.

Indemnity clauses will not necessarily give the employer complete protection. He may still be liable for claims which arise from acts or negligence for which he, or others engaged directly by him and not the contractor, are responsible.

Contractors are required by law to take out insurance to cover their liability for injury or accident to their own employees. Their public liability insurance should adequately cover the indemnity given to the employer. Fixing a realistic figure is not easy; insurance matters should be discussed with the employer at pre-tender stage, and doubtless the employer will wish to take expert advice. The relevant criteria about foreseeable risks have to be taken into account and also the fact that it may be many years before damages are awarded. It would be wise to regard a figure of £2 million as the minimum cover to be arranged under the contract. It should remain in force at least until the end of the defects liability period.

Many contractors will produce their employers' liability and public liability policies to prove compliance. Sometimes they will offer 'documentary evidence', but this will not necessarily state the exceptions and limitations (see *Schedule of insurances*).

This Volume
Fig 6.4.2 Schedule of insurances

Volume 1
Action checklist F2.1 (70)
Action checklist J2.1 (70),
J6 Initial Project Meeting
Action checklist K2.1 (70)

JCT 80

Clause 20

The contractor is required to indemnify the employer if claims arise in respect of personal injury or death. Inclusion of the words 'except to the extent that the same is due to any act or neglect of the employer' means that even if the employer is partly to blame the indemnity is not totally lost. The employer and persons employed directly by him are not the contractor's responsibility.

The contractor is also required to indemnify the employer if claims arise in respect of damage to property. The injury or damage must be due to negligence, default, omission or breach of statutory duty by the contractor or those for whom he is responsible. The employer does not totally lose the indemnity even if there was some fault on his part. The employer, persons employed directly by him and statutory undertakers are excluded.

The word 'property' does not include the works or materials on site. Parts of the works taken over under the provisions for partial possession are covered by the indemnity required under Clause 20·2.

Clause 21

The contractor is required to arrange and maintain liability insurance, and to make sure that sub-contractors are adequately covered. The limit of indemnity cover required under the contract has to be entered in the Appendix. This is the minimum required – the clause refers to the cover being 'not less than the sum stated in the Appendix'. The employer is entitled to check the contractor's insurances.

The Contractor shall be liable for, and shall indemnify the Employer ... *(Clause 20·1 and 20·2)*

... the Contractor shall take out and maintain ... insurance ... in respect of claims arising out of his liability referred to in clauses 20·1 and 20·2. *(Clause 21·1·1·1)*

... the Contractor shall ... send to the Architect for inspection by the Employer documentary evidence ... *(Clause 21·1·2)*

IFC 84

Clause 6·1

The provisions are broadly similar to those under Clause 20·1 of JCT 80.

Clause 6·2

The provisions are broadly similar to those under Clause 20·2 of JCT 80.

MW 80

Clauses 6·1, 6·2

The provisions are broadly similar to those under Clauses 20·1 and 20·2 of JCT 80, although the wording is compressed.

The employer may be liable for damage to property where there has been no negligence, no breach of statutory duty, and no default or omission by the contractor. The indemnity provided by the contractor only applies where he, the contractor, has been negligent, and his public liability policy protects him alone. Thus the employer has no protection.

Damage to adjoining property due to removal of support may result in the employer being liable for nuisance – a strict liability quite distinct from proving negligence.

In certain circumstances it is advisable for the employer to arrange special insurance to cover such risks. Such cover is usually limited, and certain types of operations or methods of working might be specifically excluded. There might also be conditions concerning such matters as the disclosure of party wall agreements, references to arbitration, and modifications to design. The insurance is intended to cover occurrences which could not be foreseen, not damage which would arise inevitably from the method of working (see *Schedule of insurances*).

This Volume
Fig 6.4.2 Schedule of insurances

Volume 1
Action checklist F2.1 (70)
Action checklist J2.1 (70),
J6 Initial Project Meeting
Action checklist K2.1 (70)

JCT 80

Clause 21·2

It must be stated in the Appendix whether this insurance is or may be required. If it may be required, the amount of the indemnity should be stated. This is to be limited to any one occurrence and with a proviso that if the indemnity is to be for an aggregate amount, this must be stated.

The contractor is not obliged to take further action unless and until instructed by the architect. If instructed, he is to take out a joint names insurance policy on behalf of himself and the employer. The employer has the right to approve the insurers and to inspect the policy and premium receipts.

Fixing the amount of indemnity requires careful thought and the architect is advised to take expert advice on behalf of the employer or to advise the employer to consult his own experts. The insurers might stipulate important provisos about the way work is to be carried out and the architect should note these carefully so as to make sure that they are followed.

> Where it is stated in the Appendix that the insurance to which clause 21·2·1 refers may be required by the Employer the Contractor shall if so instructed by the Architect take out and maintain a Joint Names Policy ... *(Clause 21·2·1).*
>
> ... insurers to be approved by the Employer and the Contractor shall send to the Architect for deposit with the Employer the policy ... *(Clause 21·2·2)*

IFC 84

Clause 6·2·4
Provisions are similar to Clause 21·2 of JCT 80.

MW 80

There are no provisions for this special insurance. If it seems to be desirable, advice should be sought from insurers. The wording of Clause 21·2 of JCT 80 might be suitable for incorporation.

Issued by:
address:

Employer:
address:

Contractor:
address:

Works:
Situated at:

Architect's instruction

Serial no:

Job reference:

Issue date:

Contract dated:

Under the terms of the above Contract, I/We issue the following instructions:

	Office use: Approx costs	
	£ omit	£ add

INSURANCE UNDER CLAUSE 21.2

Please obtain and send to us for consideration by the employer a proposal for 'joint names' insurance cover to the requirements set out in clause 21.2 of the contract, and for the amount of indemnity entered in the Appendix.

This may be offered as an extension to your annual public liability policy, but the employer reserves the right to approve the insurers.

This Instruction is issued in accordance with clause 21.2 of the contract, and the Appendix entry which states that this insurance may be required.

To be signed by or for the issuer named above.

Signed _____

Amount of Contract Sum	£
± Approximate value of previous instructions	£ _____
	£
± Approximate value of this instruction	£ _____
Approximate adjusted total	£

Distribution

☐ Employer ☐ Contractor ☐ Quantity Surveyor ☐ Services Engineer

☐ ☐ Nominated Sub-Contractors ☐ Structural Engineer ☐ File

© 1985 RIBA Publications Ltd

215

Issued by:
address:

Architect's instruction

Employer:
address:

Serial no:

Job reference:

Contractor:
address:

Issue date:

Contract dated:

Works:
Situated at:

Under the terms of the above Contract, I/We issue the following instructions:

	Office use: Approx costs	
	£ omit	£ add

'JOINT NAMES' INSURANCE POLICY: Clause 21.2 of the Contract

Take out and maintain a 'joint names' insurance policy in accordance with the attached proposal from (insurers) of (date), which has been approved by the employer.

Send us as soon as possible the policy and premium receipts, which will be deposited with the employer.

The sums of money which you have spent in this connection will be added to the contract sum.

This Instruction is issued in accordance with clause 21.2 of the contract.

To be signed by or for
the issuer named
above.

Signed _____

Amount of Contract Sum	£
± Approximate value of previous instructions	£ _____
	£
± Approximate value of this instruction	£ _____
Approximate adjusted total	£

Distribution   ☐ Employer   ☐ Contractor   ☐ Quantity Surveyor   ☐ Services Engineer

☐   ☐ Nominated Sub-Contractors   ☐ Structural Engineer   ☐ File

© 1985 RIBA Publications Ltd

The paramount obligation of the contractor is to carry out and complete the works. Unless there is something to the contrary in the contract, he must achieve this despite loss or damage to the works for whatever reason, and he must bear the cost involved.

However, it makes good commercial sense for the works and materials on site to be adequately insured, so that in the event of loss or damage there will be sufficient funds to complete the work.

A decision has to be made pre-contract about who is to be responsible for insuring the works. In some cases there is an allocation of responsibility. The person responsible for insuring the works would be liable for any shortfall. It has been common practice to require insurance for 'all risks', although this is not a precise term and usually means 'all risks with certain specified exceptions'.

The insurance should be sufficient to cover the value of full reinstatement. If there is under-insurance, any claim is likely to be scaled down in proportion. It usually costs more to reinstate a building than it costs to build it in the first place. And in times of inflation, costs might rise significantly during the progress of the works, so that cover needs to be kept under review. It is essential in any case that it operates until practical completion, and where extensions of time have resulted in an extended contract period, this fact should not be overlooked. Also, where insurance of the works is to be covered by a contractor's annual policy, it is essential to make sure that the policy is renewed at the appropriate time.

A joint names policy makes sense, because both employer and contractor need protection in the event of dispute and subsequent litigation if the works are damaged and there are allegations of negligence by either party. But note that the contract may provide that the works are at the employer's risk, whether or not damage results from the contractor's default, and the employer would therefore bear the risk of any 'excess'.

There are two important matters which are not usually covered by insurance of the works. The first is damage which arises directly from design defects. Many insurers contend that design damage is not part of the contract works insurance cover and that designers are covered by their own professional policies. The second is loss suffered by the employer when completion of the works is delayed, and the consequential extensions of time mean that the employer is unable to recover liquidated damages. Loss of profit or consequential loss of this kind needs to be covered in a separate policy. Many people in industry or commerce are protected by business-interruption policies which can be extended to include losses suffered as the result of damage to the contract works.

JCT contracts place the obligation for insuring the works upon one or other of the parties. Where the employer operates a policy of not having his buildings insured, special arrangements should be agreed before the contract is entered into (see *Schedule of insurances*).

This Volume
Fig 6.4.2 Schedule of insurances

Volume 1
Action checklist F2.1 (70)
Action checklist J2.1 (70),
J6 Initial Project Meeting
Action checklist K2.1 (70)

JCT 80

Clause 1·3

This clause defines 'Excepted Risks', for which cover is not obtainable, and 'Specified Perils' (see Clause 22C·1, Clause 25·4·3, and Clause 28·1·3·2).

Clause 22·2

This defines 'All Risks Insurance' (see Clause 22A, 22B and Clause 22C·2). Perils not specifically listed are at the contractor's risk.

Clause 22A

New buildings – the contractor is required to insure.
A joint names policy against 'all risks' is to be taken out. It should cover full reinstatement value and professional fees. It must be kept in force until practical completion.

Insurers are to be approved by both the employer and the contractor. Inspection of documentary evidence is the employer's responsibility.

Where the contractor has an annual policy, the obligation to insure the works may be met by an appropriate endorsement. The annual renewal date is to be supplied by the contractor and entered in the Appendix.

Clause 22B

New buildings – the employer to insure.
A joint names policy against 'all risks' is to be taken out. It should cover full reinstatement value and professional fees. It must be kept in force until practical completion. If there is any under-insurance, any shortfall in the cost of reinstatement (which is to be valued as a variation) must be borne by the employer.

In the private version only, the employer must be willing to produce documentary-evidence to satisfy the contractor. If he defaults, the contractor may make his own insurance arrangements and the cost is added to the contract sum.

Clause 22C·1

Existing structures – the employer to insure.
A joint names policy against 'specified perils' is to be taken out. It should cover the full cost of reinstatement, repair or replacement of the existing structure and its contents. If it proves impossible to obtain this cover, the parties must agree before entering into the contract what arrangements will be made.

In the private version only, the employer must be willing to produce documentary evidence for the contractor's inspection.

Clause 22C·2

Works in or extension to existing structures – the employer to insure.
A joint names policy against 'all risks' is to be arranged. It should cover full reinstatement value and professional fees. It must be kept in force until practical completion.

It would be sensible to arrange the insurance required under Clauses 22C·1 and 22C·2 with the same insurers.

Clause 22D

Full reinstatement value of the works does not include consequential losses and in particular the loss suffered by the employer due to delay in completing the works. It might be necessary following damage to the works to grant the contractor an extension of time (but only in respect of 'specified perils', not 'all risks' – hence vandalism, impact, theft etc are not valid reasons). If a later completion date is fixed in these circumstances, liquidated damages cannot be recovered.

Under this clause the employer may require insurance cover against this consequential loss. It must be stated in the Appendix whether insurance is or may be required. If it may be required then the period of time to be covered must be entered. The amount of the liquidated damages will also be entered in the Appendix. It is important that the figure is a genuine pre-estimate, although it is not likely to be questioned by the insurers. It might be reflected in the premium.

The contractor is not obliged to take further action unless and until instructed by the architect. If instructed, he is to obtain a quotation for the employer to consider. The contractor is then to act as further instructed and the cost of the insurance will be added to the contract sum. The policy document is to be deposited with the employer.

Clause 23·3

Insurance cover is arranged on the assumption that the contractor has exclusive possession of the site of the works. The insurers must be informed if the employer wishes to use part of the works for any purpose, including the storage of goods or materials.

If this increases the risk, an additional premium might be required. If insurance is the contractor's responsibility, the amount is added to the contract sum.

The Contractor shall take out and maintain a Joint Names Policy for All Risks Insurance ... *(Clause 22A·1)*

... the Contractor shall send to the Architect for deposit with the Employer that Policy ... *(Clause 22A·2)*

or

The Employer shall take out and maintain a Joint Names Policy for All Risks Insurance ... *(Clause 22B·1)*

The Employer shall, as and when reasonably required to do so by the Contractor, produce documentary evidence ... *(Clause 22B·2)*

or

The Employer shall take out and maintain a Joint Names Policy in respect of the existing structures ... *(Clause 22C·1)*

> (and)
>
> The Employer shall take out and maintain a Joint Names
> Policy for All Risks Insurance ... for the full reinstatement
> value of the works ... *(Clause 22C·2)*
>
> The Employer shall, as and when reasonably required to do
> so by the Contractor, produce documentary evidence ...
> *(Clause 22C·3)*
>
> Where it is stated in the Appendix that the insurance to
> which clause 22D refers may be required ... the Architect
> shall either inform the Contractor that no such insurance is
> required or shall instruct the Contractor ... *(Clause 22D·1)*

IFC 84

Clause 8·3
Specified perils are defined in this clause.

Clause 6·3
The provisions are broadly as those in Clauses 22, 22A, 22B, 22C
and 22D of JCT 80.

Clause 2·1
The employer has to pay an additional premium if he wishes to use
part of the works (as Clause 23·3 of JCT 80).

MW 80

Amendment 4:1987 to MW 80 provides a facility for the employer who wishes to have the BEC Guarantee as part of the contract. Full details of the scheme are available from *BEC Building Trust Ltd, 18 Mansfield Street, London W1M 9FG.*

Clause 6·3A
New works – the contractor to insure.
A joint names policy against perils stated in the clause is to be taken out. It should cover full reinstatement value plus professional fees and remain in force until practical completion.

Clause 6·3B
Existing structures – the employer to insure
A joint names policy against perils specified in the clause is to be taken out. This covers damage or loss to the existing structures, the contents, the new work, and site materials.

Clause 6·4
Where 6·3A applies, the contractor must produce evidence for the employer's inspection as reasonably required. Where 6·3B applies, the employer must produce evidence for the contractor's inspection.

> The Contractor shall in the Joint Names ... insure against loss and damage ... *(Clause 6·3A)*
>
> or
>
> The Employer shall in the Joint Names ... insure against loss or damage to the existing structures ... and to the works ... *(Clause 6·3B)*

Issued by:
address:

Architect's instruction

Employer:
address:

Serial no:

Job reference:

Contractor:
address:

Issue date:

Contract dated:

Works:
Situated at:

Under the terms of the above Contract, I/We issue the following instructions:

| | Office use: Approx costs | |
| | £ omit | £ add |

INSURANCE UNDER CLAUSE 22D

Obtain and submit to us for consideration by the employer a quotation for insurance on an agreed value basis in accordance with clause 22D of the contract and for the amount of liquidated damages and the period of time stated in the Appendix.

This Instruction is issued in accordance with clause 22D of the contract, and the Appendix entry which states that this insurance may be required.

To be signed by or for
the issuer named
above.

Signed _____

Amount of Contract Sum	£	
± Approximate value of previous instructions	£	
	£	
± Approximate value of this instruction	£	
Approximate adjusted total	£	

Distribution   ☐ Employer   ☐ Contractor   ☐ Quantity Surveyor   ☐ Services Engineer

☐   ☐ Nominated Sub-Contractors   ☐ Structural Engineer   ☐ File

© 1985 RIBA Publications Ltd

Fig 6.3.2 Specimen AI concerning taking out an insurance policy to cover employer's loss of liquidated damages For use with JCT 80

Issued by:
address:

Employer:
address:

Contractor:
address:

Works:
Situated at:

Architect's instruction

Serial no:

Job reference:

Issue date:

Contract dated:

Under the terms of the above Contract, I/We issue the following instructions:

	Office use: Approx costs	
	£ omit	£ add

INSURANCE UNDER CLAUSE 22D

Take out forthwith and maintain insurance in accordance with the attached quotation from (insurers) of (date), which has been approved by the employer.

Send us the policy and premium receipts as soon as possible. These will be deposited with the employer.

The sum of money which you have spent in this connection will be added to the contract sum.

This Instruction is issued in accordance with clause 22D.1 of the contract.

To be signed by or for the issuer named above.

Signed _____

Amount of Contract Sum	£	
± Approximate value of previous instructions	£	_____
	£	
± Approximate value of this instruction	£	_____
Approximate adjusted total	£	

Distribution ☐ Employer ☐ Contractor ☐ Quantity Surveyor ☐ Services Engineer

☐ ☐ Nominated Sub-Contractors ☐ Structural Engineer ☐ File

Once the insurers have accepted a claim, and unless there is anything to the contrary in the terms of the contract, the contractor is obliged to restore damaged work, to replace or repair damaged materials, and to continue to carry out and complete the works. He must do this with 'due diligence'.

Volume 1
Action checklist K2.1 (70)

The contract terms may provide for determining the contractor's employment, if it is not practicable to continue with the work following damage.

Where there is reinstatement, payment is best covered by separate reinstatement certificates. These will cover the reinstatement work only, and will cease when this work is complete. (Other work proceeding concurrently on the site will be covered by regular Interim Certificates.)

The Interim Certificate issued after the loss or damage should include the value of work properly done by the contractor which had not been certified at the date of the damage to the works. The employer does not pay twice: the contractor is paid for the reinstatement out of the insurance monies.

JCT 80

Clause 22A·4

The contractor must give written notice to the architect and the employer as soon as the loss or damage is known, with details of its extent, nature and location. As soon as the insurers have carried out an inspection, the contractor is obliged to restore, replace or repair, and to dispose of debris. The contractor is reimbursed from insurance monies paid under certificates issued at the same intervals as Interim Certificates. *If the insurance monies do not cover the cost of the work, the contractor has to bear any shortfall*. He is obliged to continue to carry out and complete the works (subject to his right to determination if the whole of the work is suspended under Clause 28·1·3·2).

Clause 22B·3

The contractor must give written notice to both the architect and the employer as soon as the loss or damage is known, with details of its extent, nature and location. As soon as the insurers have carried out an inspection, the contractor is obliged to restore, replace or repair, and to dispose of debris. The contractor is reimbursed for the work which has to be carried out. This is to be treated as a variation and valued in accordance with Clause 13·4·1. *If the insurance monies received by the employer do not cover the cost of this, then the employer has to bear the shortfall*. The contractor is obliged to continue to carry out and complete the works (subject to his right to determination if the whole of the work is suspended under Clause 28·1·3·2).

Clause 22C·4

The contractor must give written notice to the architect and the employer as soon as the loss or damage is known, with details of the extent, nature and location of the damage. Either party then has the opportunity, within 28 days of the damage occurring, to determine the employment of the contractor, subject to this action being just and equitable. Whether or not the action is just and equitable is a question which may be referred to arbitration. If there is no determination, then after the insurers have carried out an inspection the contractor is obliged to restore, replace or repair, and to dispose of debris. The contractor is to be reimbursed for the work which has to be carried out, which is to be treated as a variation and valued accordingly. *If the insurance monies received by the employer do not cover the cost of this, then the employer has to bear any shortfall.* The contractor is obliged to continue to carry out and complete the works.

... The Contractor shall forthwith give notice in writing both to the Architect and the Employer ... *(Clause 22A·4·1)*

... The Contractor with due diligence shall restore such work damaged ... *(Clause 22A·3)*

The Contractor shall not be entitled to any payment ... other than the monies under the aforesaid insurance. *(Clause 22A·4·5)*

or

... the Contractor shall forthwith give notice in writing both to the Architect and to the Employer ... *(Clause 22B·3·1)*

... the Contractor with due diligence shall restore such work damaged ... *(Clause 22B·3·3)*

The restoration, replacement or repair ... shall be treated as ... a Variation ... *(Clause 22B·3·5)*

or

... the Contractor shall forthwith give notice in writing both to the Architect and to the Employer ... *(Clause 22C·4)*

... the Employment of the Contractor ... may be determined at the option of either party ... *(Clause 22C·4·3·1)*

... the Contractor with due diligence shall restore such work damaged ... *(Clause 22C·4·4·1)*

... the restoration, replacement or repair ... shall be treated as ... a Variation ... *(Clause 22C·4·4·2)*

IFC 84

Clause 6·3A·4
The provisions are as those for Clause 22A·4 of JCT 80.

Clause 6·3B·3
The provisions are as those for Clause 22B·3 of JCT 80.

Clause 6·3C·4
The provisions are as those for Clause 22C·4 of JCT 80.

MW 80

Clause 6·3A
There is no express obligation for the contractor to inform, but this must be implied. After the insurers have carried out an inspection, the contractor is obliged to restore, replace, and dispose of debris. If the insurance monies do not cover the cost of the work, the contractor bears any shortfall.

Clause 6·3B
The contractor is not obliged to do anything until instructions are issued by the architect. The cost of work is treated as a variation and valued accordingly.

> After any inspection required ... the Contractor shall with due diligence restore or replace work or materials ...
> *(Clause 6·3A)*
>
> ... The Contractor shall not be entitled to any payment ... other than the monies received under the said insurance ...
> *(Clause 6·3A)*
>
> or
>
> ... if any loss ... occurs then the Architect shall issue instructions ... and such instructions shall be valued under clause 3·6 hereof. *(Clause 6·3B)*

Fig 6.4.1   **Specimen AI following notice of loss or damage to works**   For use with JCT 80

Issued by:
address:

Architect's instruction

Employer:
address:

Serial no:

Job reference:

Contractor:
address:

Issue date:

Contract dated:

Works:
Situated at:

Under the terms of the above Contract, I/We issue the following instructions:

	Office use: Approx costs	
	£ omit	£ add

LOSS OR DAMAGE TO WORKS

Put in hand immediately the following work:

1   Arrange and maintain security of the works and ensure that only authorised persons are allowed access.

2   Make all damaged parts of the works safe and secure.

3   Arrange protection for the works from further damage or deterioration.

4   Make any arrangements needed to assist the insurers in their inspections.

5   Ensure that vouchers and dayworks sheets for this work are checked and signed by the clerk of works before they are sent to us.

This Instruction is issued under clause 22 of the contract in response to your notice of (date) that loss or damage has occurred. The restoration and repair of the damaged work will begin after the insurers have made their inspections in accordance with the provisions of the contract.

To be signed by or for
the issuer named
above.   Signed _____

Amount of Contract Sum	£
± Approximate value of previous instructions	£ _____
	£
± Approximate value of this instruction	£ _____
Approximate adjusted total	£

Distribution	☐ Employer	☐ Contractor	☐ Quantity Surveyor	☐ Services Engineer
	☐	☐ Nominated Sub-Contractors	☐ Structural Engineer	☐ File

Schedule	MW 80	IFC 84	JCT 80	Action
Insurance against injury to persons and property				
Insurance to cover the liability of the contractor or sub-contractor against injury to persons and property – cover for any one occurrence or series of occurrences arising out of one event, for not less than the sum stated (either in the relevant clause or the Appendix to the contract).	6·2	6·11	21·1·1	*Employer* None needed. *Contractor* Arrange immediately for adequate cover. (Figure in contract is only the *minimum* required.) Send documentary evidence to architect for inspection by employer.
Special insurance against damage to property other than the works				
Insurance in respect of expense, liability, loss, claim or proceedings which the employer may incur by reason of damage to property other than the works, and where the Appendix shows that it may be required. Cover in the amount shown in the Appendix for any one occurrence or series of occurrences arising out of any one event.	NA	6·2·4	21·2·1	*Employer* Instruct contractor through architect. Approve insurance. *Contractor* Arrange immediately on receipt of Architect's Instructions the joint names cover required (usually necessary right from start of site operations). Send documentary evidence to architect for inspection by employer.
Insurance of the works by contractor against all risks				
All risks insurance of the works etc, in joint names, for full reinstatement value (to include professional fees).	NA	6·3A	22A	*Employer* Approve insurers. *Contractor* Arrange immediately for adequate cover. Supply annual renewal date if applicable. Send documentary evidence to architect for inspection by employer.
Insurance of the works by contractor against specified perils				
Insurance of the works against loss and damage by fire etc for full reinstatement value (to include professional fees).	6·3A	NA	NA	*Employer* None needed. *Contractor* Arrange immediately for adequate cover. Produce documentary evidence as required by employer.

Fig 6.4.2   Schedule of insurances (continued)

Schedule	MW 80	IFC 84	JCT 80	Action
Insurance of the works by employer against all risks				
All risks insurance of the works for full reinstatement value (to include professional fees).	NA	6·3B	22B	*Employer* Arrange immediately for adequate cover. (Note that cost of reinstatement is deemed a variation and is to be valued as such. Employer will bear excess and shortfall.) Produce documentary evidence as required by contractor. *Contractor* None needed.
Insurance of existing buildings etc by employer against specified perils				
Insurance of existing structures and contents against specified perils for full cost of reinstatement, repair or replacement.	NA	6·3C	22C	*Employer* Arrange immediately for adequate cover (see previous action note).
against all risks Insurance of new works in existing structures or extensions for full reinstatement value (to include professional fees).				*Contractor* None needed.
Insurance of existing buildings etc by employer				
Insurance against loss and damage by fire etc of existing structures and contents, and new works.	6·3B	NA	NA	*Employer* Arrange immediately for adequate cover (see previous action note). *Contractor* None needed.
Insurance against employer's loss of liquidated damages				
Insurance to cover employer's loss of liquidated damages, where Appendix shows that it may be required.	NA	6·3D	22D	*Employer* Instruct contractor through architect to obtain a quotation. Instruct on acceptance of quotation. *Contractor* When instructed by architect, obtain quotations. Arrange cover immediately if instructed to accept quotation. Send documentary evidence to architect for deposit with employer.

'Watchpoints'

Check the form of contract

* Check that the form of contract incorporates the relevant amendments relating to insurance and related liability provisions. Read the wording carefully. Have JCT Practice Note 22 at hand and make sure you read the relevant parts.

* Check that Appendix entries are complete and that the figures entered are realistic. Take expert advice or arrange for the employer to consult his own experts (eg insurance brokers). Don't slavishly follow previous entries.

Responsibility for insuring the works

* Obtain the employer's instructions about who is to accept responsibility for insuring the works. Recommend 'all risks' cover whenever this is obtainable. If the employer wishes to accept 'sole risk' (and note that these words do not appear in amended JCT contracts), make sure that he knows what this means. Remind him that the party who accepts the responsibility for insurance also carries any excess and bears any shortfall.

Special insurance cover

* Remember that for special insurance for property other than the works and for insurance against the employer's consequential loss, the contractor does nothing until instructed by you. In the case of special insurance the greatest need might be in the first weeks on site, and there might be limitations on working of which you should be aware.

* Make sure that insurance cover is sufficient to meet the full reinstatement value throughout the job (remember that costs may rise while the work is being carried out) and that cover continues if the contract period is extended.

* If the contractor insures under his annual policy, make sure the renewal date is entered in the Appendix and that cover is maintained as requested.

Check the insurance documentation

* Pass on to the employer all policies, receipts and documentary evidence received from the contractor. Check that he sends everything required by the contract. Although responsibility for approving and inspecting policies rests with the employer, you should check them carefully for yourself so that you are aware of any limitations or restrictions imposed by the insurers.

Actions in the event of loss or damage

* In the event of loss or damage check immediately with the contractor what he intends to do regarding:
  · maintaining the security and protection of the site or works;
  · removing hazards;
  · arranging for the insurers to inspect;
  · preparing a schedule of the extent of loss or damage;
  · any demolition required and removal of debris.

* It is advisable to arrange for separate accounting procedures for reinstatement work. The contractor is entitled to be paid for all work properly carried out before the damage, even if it has now been destroyed. Remember that only damages caused by specified perils can be considered for extensions of time and are grounds for determination under Clause 28 of JCT 80.

Partial possession

* Remind the employer of his responsibility for insurance following partial possession or practical completion. If the employer intends to use or occupy part of the site or works, the insurers may take a different view of the risks involved. Proper contractual procedures must be followed and the insurers must be informed.

Determination

7

'Watchpoints'

References

JCT   **Practice Note**
                       IN/1: (Determination p 6)

RIBA   **'Practice'**
                       Cash flow, profitability and insolvency (August 1984 p 3)

It is theoretically possible, although it seems seldom to have happened in building contracts, for events to make the performance of a contract impossible. In legal terms, the contract is frustrated and the parties are thereby discharged from further performance of their obligations.

It is possible for both parties who have entered into a binding contract to terminate it by agreement – a so-called bilateral discharge.

One of the parties, either through non-performance or by performing in a gravely defective manner, may be held to have repudiated the contract. However, the contract cannot be terminated unless the innocent party accepts the repudiation – he may, for example, continue to insist on his right to performance. If there is repudiation, a claim for damages will almost surely follow, although there does not seem to be any precise definition of what constitutes a repudiation.

Where the contract allows for it, either party may take action to determine. Not all building contracts include provision for determination by either party, and the terms of the particular contract are paramount. Some contracts use the word 'termination' instead of 'determination'.

The JCT forms provide for determination of the contractor's employment, not determination of the contract itself. The conditions of the contract remain in force and certain of the rights and obligations continue to have effect.

The exercise of a power to determine needs to be handled with extreme care. The grounds for determination must be established beyond doubt and the procedures in the particular contract meticulously followed. The consequences of wrongful determination could be severe and might amount to a repudiation of the contract, incurring a liability for heavy damages.

Action by the employer might arise where the employer finds it necessary to determine the employment of the contractor. Where the contractor, for good reason and on the grounds set out in the contract, elects to determine his own employment, then action is still required by the employer. The specimen letters in this chapter cover both eventualities.

Because determination is a matter which seriously affects the employer, the architect should be sure that the employer is kept fully informed about events which might lead to determination.

Volume 1
Action checklist K2.1 (70)
K7 Determining the
Contractor's Employment

JCT 80

Clause 27·1

The employer may determine the employment of the contractor if he wholly suspends the carrying out of the works without reasonable cause, if he fails to proceed regularly and diligently, if he fails to remove defective work or materials as instructed and the works are materially affected, and if he fails to comply with the assignment and sub-contracting provisions of Clause 19.

The architect may issue, or arrange for the issue of notice by registered post or recorded delivery informing the contractor that he is in default, and specifying the default. It would also be wise to remind the contractor of the possible consequences. A copy of the notice should be sent to the employer.

If the default continues for 14 days after receipt of the notice, or is repeated subsequently, the employer may determine the contractor's employment. The employer (probably through his solicitor) must give a formal notice of determination by registered post or recorded delivery.

Clause 27·2

In the event of the contractor becoming bankrupt or otherwise insolvent, his employment is automatically determined, although it may be reinstated by agreement. Meanwhile the architect should immediately take steps to secure the site and should inform the employer of all actions taken, advising him not to make any direct payments to nominated sub-contractors that may have been authorised. He should also arrange for a progress record on the contract and a financial statement to be prepared.

Clause 27·3

Note that grounds for determination by the employer also include corruption.

Clause 28A

Determination is open to either party where the whole or substantially the whole of the work is suspended for a continous period of the length stated in the Appendix for neutral causes listed as force majeure, loss or damage by specified perils and civil commotion. Note that loss or damage must be due to negligence by the main contractor or those for whom he is responsible. And under this clause, if the contractor determines his employment he is not entitled to any direct loss and/or damage caused by the determination.

> ... then the Architect may give to him (the Contractor) a notice by registered post or recorded delivery specifying the default ... *(Clause 27·1)*
>
> ... then the Employer may by notice by registered post or recorded delivery forthwith determine the employment of the Contractor ... *(Clause 27·1)*

IFC 84

Clause 7·1

The employer may determine the employment of the contractor if the contractor wholly suspends the carrying out of the works without reasonable cause, if he fails to proceed regularly and diligently, if he fails to remove defective work or materials as instructed and the works are materially affected, and if he fails to comply with the provisions relating to sub-contracting, or named persons as sub-contractors.

The architect may issue (note that IFC 84 does not specifically refer to notice by the architect) or arrange for the issue of notice by registered post or recorded delivery informing the contractor that he is in default, and specifying the default. It might be wise to remind the contractor of the possible consequences. A copy of the notice should be sent to the employer.

If the default continues for 14 days after receipt of the notice, or is repeated subsequently, the employer may determine the contractor's employment. The employer must give a formal notice of determination by registered post or recorded delivery.

Clause 7·8

Either the employer or the contractor may determine the employment of the contractor if the carrying out of the whole or substantially the whole of the works is suspended for a period of three months due to force majeure, damage by specified perils, or civil commotion.

Clause 7·2

In the event of the contractor becoming bankrupt the provisions are similar to those under Clause 27·2 of JCT 80.

> ... if the Contractor shall continue such default for 14 days after receipt of a notice ... specifying the default ... then the Employer may thereupon by notice ... determine the employment of the Contractor ... *(Clause 7·1)*

MW 80

Clause 7·1

The employer may determine the employment of the contractor if he wholly suspends the carrying out of the works without reasonable cause, if he fails to proceed regularly and diligently, or if he becomes bankrupt or otherwise insolvent.

The employer must give formal notice by registered post or recorded delivery. There are no time limits for serving notices.

> The Employer may ... by notice ... forthwith determine the employment of the Contractor ... *(Clause 7·1)*

Fig 7.1.1   **Specimen warning notice to contractor**   For use with JCT 80
specifying default

Send by Registered Post or Recorded Delivery

```
In accordance with clause 27.1 of the contract, we give notice
that you have made default in the following respect:

     (cite the relevant sub-clause number, and describe the
     default alleged)

If you continue in such default for 14 days after receipt of this
notice, or at any time repeat such default, take note that the
employer may, within 10 days of such continuance or repetition,
determine your employment under this contract.



Copy to: employer, quantity surveyor, consultants, clerk of
         works
```

Fig 7.1.2   **Specimen letter to employer**   For use with JCT 80
following continuance of default by the contractor

```
Further to the warning letter we sent to the contractor of
(date), copied to you, we regret to inform you that the
contractor has continued in the default specified. We have
received no satisfactory explanation from the contractor for this
continuance.

We consider that you now have the right to determine the
contractor's employment in accordance with clause 27 of the
contract. This is not an action to be taken lightly, and we
advise you to discuss the matter with your legal advisers as soon
as possible. We will supply any information they may require.

Under the contract only you (or legal advisers acting on your
behalf) are empowered to serve the notice of determination. It
must be sent by recorded delivery or registered post.

We remind you that in the event of determination the contractor's
liability for insuring the works ceases. You will therefore need
to arrange cover until another contractor is appointed.
```

Fig 7.1.3 **Specimen letter to contractor** For use with JCT 80
following notice of default by nominated sub-contractor

Send by Registered Post or Recorded Delivery

We have received your letter of (date), in which you allege
default by the nominated sub-contractor, (name).

In accordance with clause 35.24.4.1 of the contract, we instruct
you to serve notice upon (the nominated sub-contractor)
specifying the default to which clause 29.1 of the sub-contract
refers.

If this default continues for a further 14 days from the date
they receive your notice, you should inform us immediately.

You must wait for a further instruction from us before
determining the employment of this nominated sub-contractor.

Copy to: client, quantity surveyor, consultants, clerk of works

Fig 7.1.4   **Specimen letter to employer**   For use with JCT 80
warning of difficulties which could result in automatic
determination of the contractor's employment

Further to our telephone conversation today about the
contractor's unexplained withdrawal from site, we now understand
that he may have difficulty in continuing with the contract. We
are trying to obtain further information.

If the contractor is unable to continue because of the financial
situations described in clause 27.2 of the contract, his
employment is automatically determined (although it may be
reinstated and continued by agreement).

If automatic determination occurs, the contractor's liability for
insuring the works ceases. We suggest that you contact your
insurance advisers immediately to arrange for appropriate cover
to take effect if and when determination occurs.

We have asked the quantity surveyor to prepare a statement of
current project finances and to make further enquiries about the
contractor's financial position.

If automatic determination occurs, it will also be necessary to
secure the site and protect the works and materials. Please let
us have your formal authorisation to give instructions to this
effect.

We will keep you fully informed of developments.

Copy to: quantity surveyor, consultants

Fig 7.1.5   Specimen letter to employer   For use with JCT 80
concerning a threat by the contractor to determine his
employment

We regret to inform you that the contractor is threatening to
determine his employment under the contract. He alleges that this
is justified on the following grounds:

    (cite the sub-clause number and reason given)

Clause 28.1 of the contract sets out the rights of the contractor
in this matter, and you will see that there will be costly
consequences for you if he carries out his threat.

We suggest therefore that you should have a meeting with the
contractor and quantity surveyor as soon as possible to see
whether these difficulties can be resolved. We will gladly make
the arrangements for any meeting.

Copy to: quantity surveyor, consultants

Fig 7.1.6   Specimen letter to employer   For use with JCT 80
                     following receipt of contractor's notice of determination

We have today received from the contractor notice of his
determination of employment issued in accordance with clause 28.1
of the contract.

We suggest that you refer this notice to your solicitors at once.
We will supply any information they need.

As a result of this determination the contractor's liability for
insuring the works has ceased. If you have not already arranged
for the appropriate cover to take effect, please do so
immediately.

We need to meet you and the quantity surveyor urgently to discuss
the situation and to consider arrangements for completing the
works. The quantity surveyor will prepare a report on the state
of the work and the current financial position.

Please let us have your authorisation to give immediate
instructions to make the site secure and protect the works and
materials.

Copy to: quantity surveyor, consultants

The employer has the right to enter the site, and to employ others to complete the works. The employer is entitled to use the temporary buildings, plant, materials etc on the site owned by the contractor. This right does not automatically extend to items on hire or lease to the contractor. There might be the benefit of agreements for the supply of materials, or for work to be done under sub-contracts, but this would depend on the particular circumstances.

The architect should make immediate arrangements for site protection and security and should advise the employer to check that the works are still properly insured. Consultants, nominated sub-contractors and suppliers, statutory undertakers, and bondsmen (if relevant) should all be informed. A site survey of the works should be prepared with a schedule of works executed and defects noted, record photographs, and an inventory of temporary buildings, plant, tools and so on.

If determination has been automatic because of insolvency, an early meeting with the liquidator/receiver is advised to establish whether it is possible to reinstate the contract. The contract can be completed by reinstatement and assignment at no additional cost; a deed of assignment between employer, contractor, liquidator/receiver, and substitute contractor is drawn up. Completion can also be effected by reinstatement and novation. This usually requires conditions to be amended, resulting in extra costs. A deed of novation between employer, contractor, liquidator/receiver, and substitute contractor is drawn up.

Otherwise the works can be completed by a new contractor. The contract can be based on the original bill of quantities and a premium, approximate quantities, schedule of rates, specification or some other appropriate document. Remember that the employer has a duty to mitigate his loss as far as possible. The method of appointing the contractor for a completion contract will largely depend on the state of the work at the time of determination.

Where work has only just started, it might be convenient to negotiate with the second lowest original tenderers. Where work has proceeded for some time but is still far from complete, competitive or negotiated tenders on the original bills plus a premium might be preferred. Where work is substantially complete, a contractor appointed on negotiated rates or a daywork basis might be acceptable. Where it is a question of remedying defects, a lump sum basis or daywork rates might be appropriate. The particular circumstances of the project will be the deciding factor.

The employment of any sub-contractors is also determined when the main contractor's employment is determined. It will depend on the willingness of the parties and practical considerations whether nominated sub-contractors or suppliers are to be reappointed. If determination of the main contractor's employment is because of insolvency, the liquidator/receiver should be kept informed.

Volume 1
Action checklist K2.1 (70)
K7 Determining the
Contractor's Employment

JCT 80

Clause 27·4
Following determination, the employer may employ others to complete the works, and use all temporary buildings, plant, tools, equipment, goods and materials on the site.

The employer or the architect may also require the contractor, within 14 days of determination, to assign to the employer the benefits of any agreement for the supply of materials or goods or execution of work.

This right of assignment is only valid if the contractor is not bankrupt or otherwise insolvent. Suppliers or sub-contractors may reasonably object to any further assignment by the employer.

When the notice of determination is decided, the architect should advise the employer of the position regarding sub-contracts for materials, goods and execution of work, and the benefits which would accrue from assigning the existing agreement.

> ... the Employer may employ and pay other persons to carry out and complete the works ... *(Clause 27·4·1)*

IFC 84

Clause 7·4
Following determination, the employer may employ others to complete the works, and use any temporary buildings, plant, tools, equipment, goods and materials on site.

The employer is also entitled to purchase all materials and goods needed to carry out the works.

> ... the Employer may employ and pay other persons to carry out and complete ... *(Clause 7·4(c))*

MW 80

There are no detailed express provisions in the contract other than Clause 7·1.

Fig 7.2.1   Specimen letter to nominated sub-contractor,   For use with JCT 80
nominated supplier or statutory undertaker
following determination of the contractor's employment

```
We write to inform you that the employment of (name), the
contractor for the above project, was determined on (date). The
site has been locked and secured and access to it is prohibited.
Goods, materials, plant and equipment may not be removed from the
site without our written permission.

We will issue further instructions relating to the completion of
the work, payments and other outstanding matters as soon as
possible.


Copy to: quantity surveyor, consultants, clerk of works
```

7.3   Removal from Site

When instructed to do so, the contractor is obliged to make an orderly withdrawal from the site.

If the employer does not wish to have the use of temporary buildings, plant, tools, equipment etc then these will be included under the instruction. If the contractor does not comply, the employer may take steps to remove them and may sell any property owned by the contractor. Proceeds from the sale, less all costs incurred by the employer, are credited to the contractor.

The employer has no rights or responsibilities for plant and equipment on hire or which the contractor has bought under a hire purchase agreement.

Unfixed materials may not be removed from site without consent. It may be necessary to establish ownership where such materials have been paid for under an Interim Certificate – a supplier may claim repossession or the receiver/liquidator may dispute the fact.

Volume 1
Action checklist K2.1 (70)
K7 Determining the
Contractor's Employment

JCT 80

Clause 27·4

Following determination, the architect or employer may require the contractor to remove from the works any temporary buildings, plant, tools, equipment, goods and materials belonging to or hired by him.

The architect should advise the employer which items should be removed and which items would be useful for completing the works and should be kept on site.

The architect must give the contractor notice in writing, and the contractor must take no action until he receives the instruction. A schedule of items to be removed from the site should accompany it.

If the contractor fails to act within a reasonable time after receiving the notice, the employer has the right to remove and dispose of the contractor's property. The proceeds, less all costs, are held to the credit of the contractor.

> ... the Contractor shall as and when required in writing by the Architect ... remove from the works any temporary buildings, plant, tools, equipment, goods and materials ...
> *(Clause 27·4·3)*

IFC 84   **Clause 7·4**   247
                               The provisions are generally similar to those under Clause 27·4 of
                               JCT 80.

> ... the Contractor shall give up possession of the site ...
> *(Clause 7·4(a))*
>
> ... as and when so instructed in writing by the Architect, the
> Contractor shall remove from the works any temporary
> buildings, plant, tools, equipment ... *(Clause 7·4(b))*

MW 80   There are no detailed express provisions in the contract to cover the
                               contractor's removal from site, only the obligation to do so.

> ... the Contractor shall immediately give up possession of
> the site ... *(Clause 7·1)*

The defaulting contractor is liable for direct loss and expense sustained by the employer due to the determination. The employer will be able to recover expenditure reasonably incurred, always bearing in mind his duty to mitigate his loss.

Volume 1
Action checklist K2.1 (70)
K7 Determining the
Contractor's Employment

If determination is due to the contractor's insolvency after practical completion, additional costs incurred through making good defects and additional professional fees etc will be added to the final account for submission to the liquidator/receiver. But where the determination occurred before practical completion, a 'notional final account' is often prepared on the assumed basis of the original contractor having completed the whole job. The difference between the notional final account and the actual cost by the new or substitute contractor (plus other losses and expenses sustained by the employer) is the figure to be submitted to the liquidator/receiver.

For these purposes full and up to date records must be kept, and detailed and accurate valuations maintained.

JCT 80

Clause 27·4
The contractor is liable for the amount of expenses incurred, including direct loss and/or damage caused to the employer by the determination.

Upon completion of the works, the architect must verify the accounts within a reasonable time and certify the amount of expenses properly incurred by the employer, and the amount of any direct loss and/or damage the employer has sustained due to the determination.

Any bondsmen involved must be kept informed of all developments.

If the contractor is bankrupt or otherwise insolvent, the liquidator/receiver must be informed and kept fully informed pending the appointment of a new contractor to complete the works, and throughout the completion contract.

When the works are finally complete, a detailed account should be drawn up (by the architect or otherwise) of all resulting building costs, including the employer's direct and legal costs (eg any adjustment of insurance, site protection measures, extra administrative costs), and additional professional fees and expenses. The account should be consolidated into a comprehensive statement and must be agreed with the liquidator/receiver.

The basis for calculating the final settlement is the difference between the notional final account of the original contractor and the actual cost of completing under a new contract.

First,   add together

> (a) the amount paid to the original contractor up to the point of determination;
> (b) the amount paid to the substitute contractor up to completion; and
> (c) the direct costs to the employer of the determination.

The total is £X.

Second,   establish the notional final account of the original contractor, giving a total of £Y.

Third,   compare the figures £X and £Y to establish the final costs which have accrued as a result of the determination.

The difference is the figure payable by the contractor to the employer or vice versa.

... the Contractor shall allow or pay to the Employer ... the amount of any direct loss and/or damage caused to the Employer by the determination ... *(Clause 27·4)*

... the Architect shall certify the amount of expenses properly incurred by the Employer and the amount of any direct loss and/or damage caused to the Employer by the determination ... *(Clause 27·4·4)*

IFC 84

Clause 7·4
The provisions are generally similar to those under Clause 27·4 of JCT 80.

MW 80

There are no provisions in the contract setting out the action to be taken, although Clause 7·1 refers to the fact that the employer is not obliged to make further payments to the original contractor until the works have been completed.

The outbreak of hostilities and war are events which could frustrate a building contract and lead to determination. The contract may set out what is to happen in such an event. Hostilities are defined as events involving the general mobilisation of the armed forces, whether or not war has been declared.

JCT 80

Clause 32

Either party may notify determination of the employment of the contractor at any time by registered post or recorded delivery. The notice shall not be issued until after 28 days from the date of the order for general mobilisation or after practical completion, unless the works have sustained war damage.

The architect may, within 14 days of the notice of determination, issue instructions for protecting the works. This is to be valued as a variation.

> ... then either the Employer or the Contractor may at any time ... forthwith determine the employment of the Contractor ... *(Clause 32·1)*
>
> ... the Architect may ... issue instructions to the Contractor requiring the execution of such protective work as shall be specified therein ... *(Clause 32·2)*

IFC 84

There are no express provisions in this contract to deal with hostilities.

MW 80

There are no express provisions in this contract to deal with hostilities.

The expression 'war damage' is defined in the *War Damage Act 1943*. It includes damage as a direct result of action by the enemy, and damage occurring as a result of action taken by a proper authority. Some building contracts contain provisions which state what is to happen in the event of war, otherwise war might be held to have frustrated the contract.

JCT 80

Clause 33

In the event of war, damage to the works or to unfixed materials or goods on site must be disregarded in calculating the amounts payable to the contractor. The architect may issue instructions concerning the removal of debris and damaged work and the erection of protective work. The contractor must make good the damage and proceed to carry out and complete the works. The architect must fix a later completion date.

If a determination notice is served under Clause 32, then the provisions of this clause apply also.

... the Architect may issue instructions requiring the Contractor to remove and/or dispose of any debris and/or damaged work and/or to execute such protective work as ... specified. *(Clause 33·1·2)*

... the Contractor shall reinstate ... and shall proceed with carrying out and completion ... *(Clause 33·1·3)*

... the Architect shall in writing fix such later completion date ... *(Clause 33·1·4)*

IFC 84

There are no express provisions in this contract to deal with war damage.

MW 80

There are no express provisions in this contract to deal with war damage.

Checking tenders

* Care taken at the outset can reduce the risk of trouble later. Check tender lists and use fair tendering methods. Bonds can mitigate the impact of insolvency; if they are difficult to obtain, be warned – there may be some good reason. If the employer wants reassurance about the financial viability of firms, define clearly the extent of any vetting you are able or prepared to make. Scrutinise tender prices, particularly if they seem out of line with previous performance.

Maintain records

* Checklists regularly used throughout the tendering and contract stages can help to detect troubles. Properly maintained records of all significant events, dates, and parties involved may later prove invaluable.

Determination

* A notice of determination is often countered by an allegation of repudiation. It's better to get it right first time.

Grounds for determination

* Grounds for determination by the employer must be clearly established. Work must be suspended 'wholly'. Failure to proceed regularly and diligently is extremely difficult to substantiate. Check with the employer before taking any action, and advise him to take legal advice.

The warning notice

* Check who is to issue the warning notice under the contract. It is usually, but not always, the architect. Follow the procedures for delivering the notice exactly. Notice only takes effect from the date it is received.

Signs of insolvency

* Keep a wary eye open for tell-tale signs of insolvency. You may notice that progress slows down, work becomes slack and defective, or plant is suddenly removed from site. There may be complaints by sub-contractors about late payment, confidential enquiries from suppliers, changes in site supervisory staff etc.

* If determination is due to the contractor's insolvency, take immediate steps to protect the employer's interests. Start by assuming that everything on site is owned by the employer. Make sure the site is secure: check fences, fit new padlocks etc. See that works and materials are protected from the weather. Stop all certificates and advise the employer to hold all monies. Arrange for a presence on site such as a clerk of works or personnel from a security firm. Inspect the state of the work and prepare reports and inventories, take photographs and so on. Find out who is to be the liquidator/receiver. Inform any bondsmen of the situation.

'Watchpoints'

Reinstatement

* Arrange to meet the liquidator/receiver to establish whether reinstatement of the contract is worth considering. But bear in mind that the liquidator/receiver may be primarily interested in raising as much money as possible from the contract in the minimum time. Standards may suffer and the morale of the work force sink.

New contract for completion

* The basis for appointing a new contractor to complete the works will be largely influenced by the state of the work when determination occurred, and how much remains to be done.

* It is important to keep the liquidator/receiver fully informed during the completion stage. No direct payments for amounts outstanding at the time of determination should be made without his agreement.

* The employer is not bound to make any further payment to the defaulting contractor until the works are complete and the extent of the loss and expense is known. This will probably entail a claim by the employer against the contractor.

Appendices

A   Preparing the Documents

1   Both parties should enter into a contract on the basis of a complete set of documents each of which has been completed as necessary.

2   A letter may be sent to the selected tenderer informing him of the decision to accept his tender. This letter should state that a contract will not exist until the documents have been prepared and executed by the parties. It is then important to make sure that execution of the contract takes place before the date agreed for possession to avoid possible allegations of frustration.

3   Where for some good reason there is insufficient time for the documents to be prepared before work begins, a letter accepting the selected tender may be sent. Once in the post, such a letter establishes a contractual relationship; it should therefore be sent by recorded delivery. The letter should inform the contractor that the employer is entering into the contract as intended and described in the tender documents, and that formal documents will follow by a specific date. There would then be an enforceable obligation to enter into a formal contract and the documents should be produced as quickly as possible.

Volume 1
Action checklist
F2.1 (20), (70)
F5 Tendering Procedures –
Documentation

Action checklist J2.1 (70)
J3 Assembling Production
Information

1   The Agreement between the employer and the contractor should be dated and reflect the correct titles and addresses of the parties. Normally the addresses will be those to which notices, instructions, certificates etc are to be sent. If either party wishes to have all contractual communications sent to a different address, this should be recorded in the contract documents.

2   The Recitals set out the facts on which the Agreement is based, and start with the customary word 'whereas'. The description of the intended works may be brief, but it should be clear and adequate. For example, 'constructing a factory and ancillary external works' or 'carrying out alterations to a bank' are clear enough for purposes of identification. The location of the site should also be conveyed precisely in a few words.

3   The name and address of the architect is to be entered in the Recitals and in Article 3. The inclusion of the name in two places takes care of the possibility that the architect appointed under the building contract may not be the same person who was appointed to prepare the design.

Extract from RIBA Practice Note, June 1980

'... It is important to the parties to a contract that the body directly responsible should be identified. As a general rule it is not appropriate for an individual to be named even though he be chief officer, partner or otherwise acting as a principal. In the opinion of the Practice Committee the appropriate name to be inserted in the Articles of Agreement for a private firm of architects is the firm itself, and for a public authority that authority's Department of Architecture. In the case of industrial and commercial organisations employing in-house architects, the name to be used will depend on the particular structure of the in-house office. Where the organisation has its own Architects' Department, this Department should be named. Otherwise the title of the official concerned, eg Chief Architect, should be used and not the name of the individual ...'. (Obviously this advice will not apply where client bodies have appointed an individual rather than the practice as architect, but it should be regarded as the general rule.)

4   The drawings which show the works need to be clearly identified. To avoid any risk of discrepancy, they should be those used for preparing the contract bills, specification or schedules of work as appropriate. Requirements might be met by including the site plan (taking care to show the physical boundaries of the works – particularly if they form part of a larger complex), general arrangement plans, sections and elevations, and any details necessary for the purposes of tendering. If the quantity of drawings is greater than can be described within the space available on the contract form, the words 'as in the attached list' may be inserted and a list headed 'Contract Drawings' be fixed securely to the page containing the relevant Recital. Drawings should be indentified beyond all doubt by giving the correct number and issue affix (eg 261/32e). It might be worth using a

rubber stamp to endorse each copy of contract drawings, bills, and any other written material which is to be incorporated as part of the contract. For example: 'This is one of the contract documents referred to in the contract between .... (Employer) and .... (Contractor) and signed hereunder (by both parties)'.

5   Some forms of contract include optional ways of settling disputes. The building industry has always preferred arbitration. The JCT forms of contract make no provision for litigation as an agreed alternative, although both JCT 80 and IFC 84 provide for disputes to be referred to the High Court under arbitration procedures. Care should be taken that any options selected (such as 'joinder') reflect the intentions of the parties and are clearly shown in the Appendix.

1 Where alternative contract provisions are to be deleted (an action not now required in the majority of current JCT forms of contract) this should be done clearly in the text of the document and should be initialled by the parties.

Whether options clauses are to apply or not should be clearly indicated in the Appendix.

2 Alterations to the text are possible, if that is what the parties want. They should be clearly indicated in the text of the document and initialled by the parties. They might be indicated at the time of tendering.

The conditions in standard forms of contract are often complex and inter-related. Even apparently innocuous alterations to a clause can affect or call into question other parts of the contract. Conditions should not be amended without considerable care and thought, and never without taking legal advice.

The NJCC has expressed its concern over unnecessary amendments in its *Procedure Note 2*. It is essential in the interests of good practice and economic building that amendments are kept to a minimum.

3 *Both JCT 80 (Clause 2·2·1) and IFC 84 (Clause 1·3) provide that the printed conditions of the contract take precedence over any typed or written words in other documents.* Therefore any additional articles, conditions or amendments must not be left to the specification or to the preliminaries section of a bill of quantities, but must be properly incorporated in the actual articles or conditions.

4 Both JCT 80 and IFC 84 have an Appendix. In the interests of accuracy, entries should be copied direct from the tender documents. Full information concerning matters to be included in the Appendix should be given at the time of tendering.

Where bills of quantities apply, the quantity surveyor is required under the *Standard Method of Measurement* to recite the clause headings of the contract conditions to give tenderers an opportunity to price those conditions which may carry financial implications. Where there are no bills of quantities, a corresponding section in the specification or schedules of work should give such information for tenderers.

5 The following notes may be helpful when completing the Appendix:

Arbitration
Both JCT 80 and IFC 84 provide for related disputes involving nominated or named sub-contractors to be joined in arbitration under the main contract.

Both JCT 80 and IFC 84 require a decision about who is to appoint the arbitrator; the nature of the work will obviously influence this. Arbitration is subject to the JCT Arbitration Rules, which are published separately. The parties agree at the outset

Volume 1
Action checklist
F2.1 (20), (70)
F5 Tendering Procedures –
Documentation

Action checklist J2.1 (70)
J3 Assembling Production
Information

that there will be reference to the High Court on points of law as provided for under the Arbitration Act 1979.

Date of Possession
The contractor should be allowed adequate time to mobilise resources and make proper arrangements. The employer should be certain that the site can be given into his possession on the date entered (Clause 23·1 of JCT 80; Clause 2·1 of IFC 84).

Date of Completion
This is the day by which the contractor is to hand over the works, having achieved practical completion. It must be realistically attainable and accurately placed (Clause 23·1 of JCT 80; Clause 2·1 of IFC 84).

Deferment of Possession
Options which were previously only included in IFC 84 are now included in JCT 80. They are advisable in all circumstances where absolute certainty cannot be guaranteed. The period should not exceed six weeks (Clause 23·1·2 of JCT 80; Clause 2·2 of IFC 84).

Liquidated Damages
The sum must be properly assessed and entered, otherwise the employer's right to deduct damages may be impaired. The prior issue of a Certificate of Non-completion is a requirement. The rate can be entered as an amount per week or month. It refers to non-completion of the whole works, and care is therefore needed where there is phased or sectional completion, for which the Sectional Completion Supplement is available (Clause 24·2 of JCT 80; Clause 2·7 of IFC 84).

Defects Liability Period
If the period is other than six months, the time should be entered. As a rule, avoid any attempt to introduce different periods (such as six months for building, twelve months for heating installations) in the same contract. If twelve months is desirable, then apply it to the contract *in toto* (Clause 17·2 of JCT 80; Clause 2·10 of IFC 84).

Period of Interim Payments
One month is traditional and convenient, but otherwise the period should be stated. If stage payments are thought preferable by the parties, then the stages should be clearly described (Clause 30·1·3 of JCT 80; Clause 4·2 of IFC 84).

Period of Final Measurement
This item appears in the Appendix to IFC 84 only.

If other than six months, a time should be stated. This is the period within which the quantity surveyor must complete measurement and valuation of all matters affecting the final cost – the adjusted contract sum. In large contracts, or ones where substantial remeasurement might be anticipated, six months may seem insufficient; periods of up to twelve months are acceptable where circumstances warrant it (Clause 4·5 of IFC 84).

Insurance

The maximum indemnity provided by the contractor's public (or third party) liability insurance should be stated. This will not be the extent of the contractor's liability, but the extent of the contractual obligation to insure in the interests of the employer (Clause 21·1·1 of JCT 80; Clause 6·2·1 of IFC 84).

Percentage to cover Fees

Professional fees, which include VAT, could be a significant part of the cost of rebuilding after damage. All professionals likely to be concerned should be included. Insurers will need to know the level of fees before underwriting the risk. It is better to overestimate than underestimate, as the premium is not significantly increased (Clause 22A of JCT 80; Clause 6·3A·1 of IFC 84).

6   MW 80 has no Appendix, but requires appropriate entries in certain clauses. These include commencement and completion dates (Clause 2·1); damages for non-completion (Clause 2·3); defects liability period (Clause 2·5); retention percentage (Clause 4·2); Final Certificate period (Clause 4·4); and professional fees percentage (if Clause 6·3A is to apply).

1   The formalities of the contract agreement should be completed before work starts on site.

Volume 1
Action checklist J2.1 (70)

2   The Articles of Agreement are normally sent first to the contractor, accompanied by the drawings listed in the Recitals and the other contract documents as appropriate. Pencil in a cross to indicate where the contractor is to sign (usually in the lower set of spaces). Documents returned by the contractor should be examined carefully to see that they have been completed properly, as requested in the covering letter.

3   The documents should then be passed to the employer with a covering letter requesting him to date the Articles. Documents returned from the employer should be examined carefully to see that they have been completed properly.

4   Instead of signing separately, the parties may agree to meet at some convenient place and complete the execution of the contract in each other's presence.

5   If the contract is under hand, only the signatures of both parties are necessary. The signatures of witnesses – desirable, though not a legal necessity – confirm the existence of the agreement.

6   If the contract is under seal, then appropriate wording should be used for the attestation clause. Special wording may be required depending on the Memorandum or Standing Orders of an authority or corporate body.

The fact that a main contract is under hand or under seal does not necessarily mean that sub-contracts or collateral agreements must be similarly executed. However, thought should be given to this matter so as to avoid confusion and unnecessary complications and costs.

Since the *Finance Act 1985*, stamp duty is no longer payable on contracts under seal. It is only when they are complicated by other matters such as conveyances or leaseback that they may still need to be stamped. In such cases the architect might advise the employer to consult his own solicitor. If in doubt, draft documents may be sent for comment to *The Controller of Stamps, Central Information Section, Bush House, South West Wing, Strand, London WC2B 4QN.*

7   The contract as a legal instrument has been executed when it has been signed, or signed and sealed; as an undertaking, when the services have been performed and the works properly done and paid for.

It will be stated in the contract conditions who is to have custody of the original contract documents – usually the employer (except for the Private Edition of JCT 80, which designates the architect or the quantity surveyor). The documents should be kept in a secure fireproof place.

Copies of the contract documents should be suitably endorsed – for example, 'This is a certified copy of the Agreement dated ... between ... and signed ... (Architect)' – and given to the contractor. The architect would be wise to keep another complete set in the office safe.

Bibliography

Contract Law

Duncan Wallace I.N.
Hudson's Building and Engineering Contracts
10th edition with Supplement
Sweet & Maxwell 1970

Keating D.
Building Contracts
4th edition with Supplements
Sweet & Maxwell 1978

JCT 80

Parris J.
The Standard Form of Building Contract: JCT 80
BSP Professional Books 1988

Powell-Smith V.
The Standard Form of Building Contract 1980 Edition
IPC Business Press 1983

IFC 84

Jones N.F., Bergman D
The JCT Intermediate Form of Building Contract
Collins 1985

Cox S.H.
The architect's guide to the JCT Intermediate Form of Building Contract (IFC 84)
Second edition
RIBA Publications 1988

MW 80

Chappell D., Powell-Smith V.
JCT Minor Works Form of Contract
Architectural Press 1986

Audas J.M.
A Builder's Guide to the Agreement for Minor Buildings Works
CIOB 1981

Clamp H.
The Shorter Forms of Building Contract
Second edition
BSP Professional Books 1988

Contract Administration

Powell-Smith V., Sims J.H.
Building Contract Claims
Granada 1983

Powell-Smith V., Sims J.H.
Contract Documentation for Contractors
Collins 1985

Madge P.
A guide to the indemnity and insurance aspects of building contracts
RIBA 1985

Madge P.
A concise guide to the JCT 1986 insurance clauses
RIBA 1987

Cecil R.
Professional Liability
Second edition
Architectural Press 1986

Powell-Smith V., Chappell D.
Building Contract Dictionary
Architectural Press 1985

The Architect as Arbitrator
Revised R. J. M. Johnstone
RIBA Publications 1987

Volume 1: Job Administration

Contents

Preface
The Fifth Edition
How to use Volume 1: Job Administration
Plan of Work

Volume 1: Job Administration

Contents

Contents

Job Record: A list of the forms

JR1   Record of commission
JR2   Register of files
JR3   Design team information
JR4   Services and fees agreed
JR5   Allocation of office resources
JR6   Project costs chart
JR7   Key project actions (PoW Stages)
JR8   Project progress chart
JR9   Record of consents
JR10 Outline of project requirements
JR11 Rooms/spaces/activities schedule
JR12 Room/area schedule
JR13 Building elements schedule
JR14 Design data
JR15 Calculation sheet
JR16 Survey information
JR17 Documents relevant to surveys
JR18 Schedule of condition
JR19 Party wall agreements
JR20 Cost plan
JR21 Supplement to cost plan
JR22 Information for bills of quantities/specification (preliminaries)
JR23 Information for bills of quantities/specification (preambles)
JR24 Information for bills of quantities/specification (specification)
JR25 Schedule of work required
JR26 Building contract information
JR27 List of potential contractors
JR28 Tender documents issued
JR29 Sub-contractors' and suppliers' tenders
JR30 Appointed contractors, sub-contractors, suppliers
JR31 Architect's Instructions issued
JR32 Record of defective work
JR33 Record of site delays observed
JR34 Schedule of claims by contractor
JR35 Defects reported after practical completion
JR36 Record of completed project
JR37 Assessment of project
JR38 Register of drawings and issue
JR39 Record of drawings received